The GRAPES of Ralph

WINE ACCORDING TO
RALPH STEADMAN

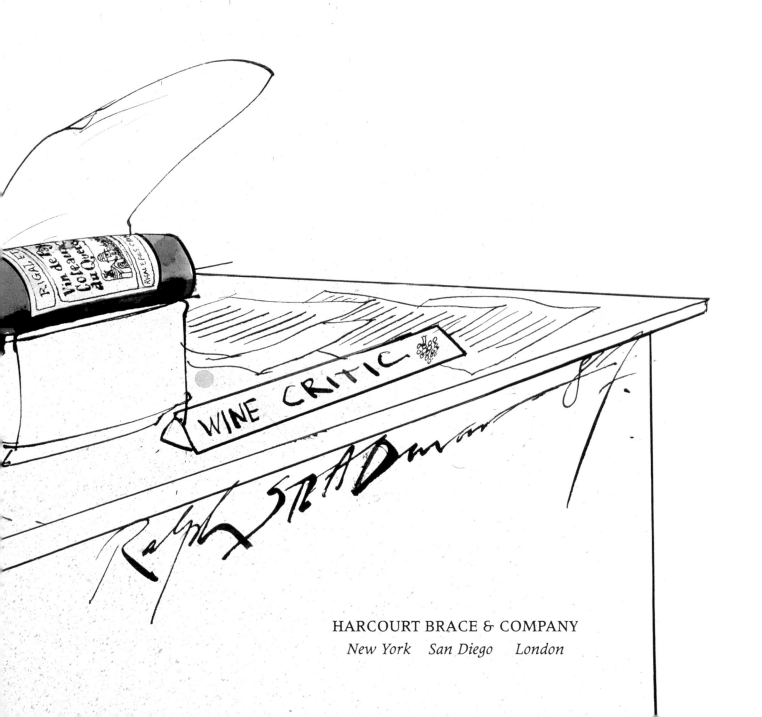

HARCOURT BRACE & COMPANY
New York   San Diego   London

Acknowledgements

My thanks to:

IAN CRAIG, the art director of this book, who came when I called because he laughs when I laugh, but thinks when I don't think, and brings together all the disparate elements that I have at hand but cannot see. He is only a little Scotsman, balding, like me, but unlike me, not balded. For this, I estimate him. He is more than I will ever be, at this point. I cannot see the wood for the barrels. He can.

ANDREW JEFFORD, my editor, who drove my prose on to be my own and not the wafflings of those who know best. In spite of my protestations he has had the professional courage to say 'No!'. My readers, he told me, have the right to expect more. He is right and his reputation deserves my acknowledgement. He has guided me through many misconceptions and driven me to distraction and near rebellion. His authority is well placed and if this book sounds a bit authentic I owe it all to Andrew, but he does remind me of my old headmaster who was an absolute bastard.

GORDON KERR, my partner in wine, the arch architect of the whole journey. Gordon, through some festering brain fever, thought it a good idea that I should go forth and see. He has suffered the slings and arrows of such outrageous fortune that even 'Omelette' is too good a name for Shakespeare's famous play. Thankfully, Gordon loves omelettes, not because he loves them, but because he hates meat and there is no alternative. Likewise, he loves me, not because he loves me, but because he hates advertising, and I hate it more than anyone. And there's the rub. Nobody is trying to sell you anything. You exist to make up your own mind, if you have one. If you haven't, I am not even going to go into it. I pity you, and sometimes I even pity Gordon, so don't even feel sorry for youself. I hate self-pity and I have watched Gordon wretching in a miasma of self-denigration. And he's a Scotsman too. But he's not that little. For four years he has been given his head—and expects it on a platter through the door at any moment.

ODDBINS, without whom, or which, none of us could survive. Let's face it. The bright lights of a hideously painted shop front would not be the same if it were not for the hideously painted shopfronts of every single branch in the country. It makes you think, and when you do, you have to ask, and the next thing you know, you're involved.

DEREK MORRISON, Oddbins MD, a generous tyrant of irascible yet thoughtful appreciation, who knows bugger-all about art but knows what's good for him—and it shows.

ANNA, my wife, who has accompanied me on every wine trip I have made. Not because I asked her to, but because I demanded her company. We have shared the experience, so don't try and bloody well catch her out with some obscure wine or something, or even try to get her pissed. She can drink us all under the table. She is elegant, and lovely, perceptive and gentle, but suffers no fools gladly, not even me.

DENISE BATES, who orchestrated this imbalance and allowed it to wet itself beneath the broad multi-coloured umbrella of the blessed publishers who always win in the end, whatever they let you do. May she always follow her heart and let things happen before her very eyes.

Text copyright © 1992 Ralph Steadman
Illustrations © 1992 Ralph Steadman

Printed in Dubai
G F E D C B

CONTENTS

1   BULGARIA   9

The traveller harvested the grapes and placed them all in the vat. He disrobed, climbed into the liquifying fruit and wallowed awhile. . . . He had at last found what he had been looking for, though previously there had been no rhyme or reason for his restless ways.

2   FRANCE   10

I tried desperately to savour the first taste on my tongue, but thirst got the better of me and I gulped a mouthful which burst inside me like a warm sensuous bomb. I followed it with a piece of black bread and thought only of France and the sheer joy of booze at the right moment.

3   GERMANY   56

A very rare occurrence, this, but come a heatwave in the middle of December, the odd shrivelled bits of grape left hanging on, after all possible variations of harvests have been plundered and exploited, explode with rich puscillating squelches and oozing promise to create a festival of rich syrupy Grossetrocken or Dribbling Noble Rotty Grot.

4   PORTUGAL   98

Since Port comes from Portugal, reasoned ex-British Consul Flight Lieutenant Buffy Bosford, why not a drink called Brit from Britain?

5   LANZAROTE   120

Apart from that I know nothing, except that the wine produced from the grapes is called La Grippa. It has a volcanic edge, bores holes in the back of eyeballs and drives men into the arms of strange women who wait like traffic wardens at a rock-concert parking frenzy.

6   ITALY   122

As soon as the wine has entered into the stomach it commences to swell up and boil over; and then the spirit of that man commences to abandon his body, and rising as though towards the sky it reaches the brain, which causes it to become divided from the body; and so it begins to infect him and to cause him to rave like a madman; and so he perpetrates irreparable crimes, killing his own friends.

7   AUSTRALIA   146

Barossa Pearl ran a Catholic soup kitchen for down-and-out gold prospectors while her husband, Archbishop Connemara, a Benedictine, roamed the outback on horseback preaching the evils of abstinence and administering communion wine as an answer to everything from dingo bite to damnation.

8   CALIFORNIA   184

Robert Louis Stevenson spent his honeymoon in the region with his new wife Fanny, and Calistogans declare with pride that he wrote 'And the wine is bottled poetry' about their very wines. I think he actually said 'And their wines are bottled properly.'

9   PERU   208

I was led to believe that they were Peruvian vineyards, but from our flying altitude they looked rather light and more like asparagus beds.

10   CHILE   210

So that's where they go in the winter time, these shadowy figures who feed the strife and tragedy of others. They lurk with elegant impunity at tasting lunches in dreamlike splendour.

The name of the Gregorian ritual is given to the ceremonies which Pope Gregory I forced to be observed from 590 A.D. in the Church of Rome with regard to the Liturgy, the administration of the sacraments and the benedictions, as laid down in the book entitled *Gregorianum Sacramentarium*. It was, in fact, an editing job on the chants of St Ambrose who carefully avoided melodies used previously in pagan worship, in an attempt to avoid calling back the thoughts and pleasant memories of Christians to a worship recently abandoned but still partly practised. Gregory introduced new tonal scales to Ambrose's more basic Greek system of tetrachords, adding his 'plagal' scales to the acknowledged Ambrose 'authentic' scales, adding letters of the alphabet to each tone in the eight scales. The chant is unaccompanied music and can be of any length simply because a single note can be repeated for any number of words in a line, provided you give yourself a pause occasionally to breathe in, and take a sip of the new vintage:

Oh, yeah, bless my vines into the ground today, oh, yeah (SIP)

And give them all the sustenance and support they are going to need, the weather being what it is and all, the ozone layer and all that global warming, oh, oh, oh, oh, yeah (BREATHE)

Guide them along the wires

Guide them, guide them, guide them

Alleluia, guide them (SIP)

Keep them free from nasty bugs like those awful things that eat the roots (BREATHE)

Phylloxera! Phylloxera! Phyllox-e-e-e-e-rall-alleluah! (SIP)

Alleluia! Alleluia! Alleluia—Phyllox-e-r-a! (SIP)

Help us find a (BREATHE) cure to purge the earth of all such plagues (SIP) like the one I just me-e-unn-tioned (SIP)

And give us rain and shine in useful measure and not all those unexpected droughty periods, not to mention those late frosts (SIP) which wreak more havoc than you probably realise (SIP and BREATHE) making a mockery of nature's natural abundance (SIP) and our hard work (SIP-SUCK-SIP)

Come off it, God, come off it

Come off-off-off it, God (GULP). (These last lines can be chanted as a chorus between your various requests and pleas for mercy, or between SIPS and SUCKS.)

The advantage of the Gregorian Wine Chant is that you can adapt it to suit your own needs and your own despair.

Introduction

I must have been associated with wine and wine-making for much longer than I realised. My mother mentioned one day, in a fit of memory, that she and my father used to go along to Water-worths, a greengrocer in the market town of Abergele in North Wales and fill two large bags each with bruised and 'slightly off' grapes for sixpence 'because they make better wine'.

It all came flooding back. The demijohns, earthenware jars, hydrometers, specific gravity testers, rubber corks, fermentation locks, isinglass, sodium metabisulphite tablets, the mesmeric gloop-gloop from beneath a huddle of blankets in the corner of the living room as the new brew of the season got up steam from a variety of fruit and veg, fermenting like bacchanalian gods at an orgy. Anything perishable was fair game. Tea leaves, rose petals, rosehips, blackberries, sprouts, parsnips, melons, potatoes, rice, apple peel, nettles, carrots, peas, oranges and lemons, plums, apricots, cucumbers, pomegranates. Cabbage was tried once but that got the raspberry from everyone and was never tried again. Neither were mushrooms.

The range of bottles used to siphon off the liquid without disturbing the precipitated must would have impressed a medieval alchemist, and the winemaking techniques and their astounding results confound an industrial chemist.

When the wine was bottled after fermentation my father would tie the corks down with hairy packing string and store them under the stairs in

case they exploded, which occasionally happened in hot weather, in the middle of the night as often as not, particularly when there was a full moon. Strange. I was thrown in at the deep end. I was invited, along with my sister and any visiting relations, to sample them all but not too much— 'in case you get a liking for it'.

My favourite, and the most agreeable among a weird variety of colours ranging from murky brown (nettles) to deep purple (beetroot), was elderberry, a wonderful bedtime sleeping draught served hot with a spoonful of honey. It was the one that looked most like real wine and made me feel very grown up and probably drunker than I realised.

The fact that I wasn't poisoned was probably my lucky break and not even a calculated risk by my mother and father, who loved me at least half as much as their new-found obsession for experimentation in this most rural of arts. I am tempted to believe that seeking out and consuming edible toadstools would have been a safer pursuit. Though, as my mother says, 'we're still alive to tell the tale'. My father died aged 92 and my mother is 87, though she prefers a drop of whisky to nettle wine these days 'to keep the tubes open'.

About five years ago the British chain of wine merchants, Oddbins, asked me (in what must have been a moment of divine inspiration) if I could produce about ten drawings on the subject of wine. It struck a chord with my early life quite subconsciously, and five years later I feel as though the subject of wine is now a life study for me, laced with a maverick's love of individual experience.

Goaded by a pathological hatred of puritan ethics and a love of something which is an art as much as a science, I embraced the subject with the intensity of a Moonie convert. Anything viney engages my interest immediately and I have been privileged to visit and talk with some great wine-makers in both hemispheres. I don't care much for the mystique surrounding the wine trade any more than I care for the plumber's claim that pipes are far too mysterious a subject for the layman to understand. However I do go along with the belief that grapes, soil, microclimates, techniques and the vagaries of weather are so diverse from one year to the next that it takes a real artist, with the soul of Faust, to cheat the devil and produce a wine so fine as to deny any one else's attempt to do the same. The essential qualities are passion, natural cunning and an individual's mad impulse to juggle the odds to create a masterpiece of pure balance and delicate complexity.

It is the artist in me that responds to such a challenge and I salute the masters of winemaking. At the same time, I have also put up my own defences against the sheer bewildering expertise of it all as a hedge against the charlatan and the manipulator, fully aware that we, the punters who would feign to be experts, are but children in their hands.

My book touches on all aspects and all pitfalls. It is one man's excursion into an Aladdin's cave of magical processes, elegant plumage, the mould of tradition and cool damp cellars, personal convictions, cant, elitism, sharp practice, nonsense and, above all, the individual bouquet of that finely crafted raw material known as an excellent vintage—the only decent reason for putting a year on a bottle of wine in the first place.

Each of my experiences has been a learning process and in each case I have tried to respond in a way which suits the indigenous character of the areas visited. I haven't been everywhere: who has? Perhaps, though, I have been to enough places to realise that two lifetimes are required to get to grips with the whole thing. Look upon this book as a light-hearted tasting of a rich and time-honoured subject. It might intrigue the novice as it does me, and it might amuse the expert. *They* may even learn something. If you learn only one thing, learn to avoid those chintzy places that serve you the wine diagonally in a fancy basket lined with a napkin. They are probably charging too much for the wine and relying on your earnest desire to look overly sophisticated and pretend to know what you are doing.

Wine is far too noble, patient and even courageous a pursuit for such phoney elegance. From one year to the next, a vineyard can live and die and along with it the reputation it may have taken generations to build.

It's a privilege to drink good wine. We should treat it with respect and savour every drop, like experts.

Ralph STEADman
KENT 1st August 1992

BULGARIA

Grape juice was poured into a vat lined with the aged scum of ageless plunderers, who travelled on, leaving behind them thicker scum.

Hardened by the sun over 2,000 years, it lay untouched for another 2,000 of the same until one day, a thirsty traveller passed by and found the fetid, hardened and time-beaten vat, rotten where the wood was dry but hard like iron where it had been impregnated by grape juice. The scum had flaked into obscurity with the years and 1000000,000000,000000.333 recurring ergs of infinite energy, from the pitiless sun.

There was just enough of the vat left for the traveller to take a bath, but there was no water, only grapes dripping with juice on vines gnarled in cracked earth, gasping for nothing but a use.

The traveller harvested the grapes and placed them all in the vat. He disrobed, climbed into the liquifying fruit and wallowed awhile. His mighty body felt refreshed as he lay in the juices crushed beneath him. He began to feel hungry and started to eat the grapes floating around him, which assuaged the initial pangs of hunger and quenched his thirst.

Gradually, he began to feel drowsy, and in time he fell asleep. When he awoke the juice he lay in was bubbling furiously all about him. He breathed in deeply and filled his lungs with a pungent aroma which forced him to cough and rise from where he lay. Although sticky, he was clean and felt a strong sense of well-being about his person. He watched the bubbling liquid day and night as a new scum formed about its rim, and then its middle, forming a crown to fit a king of high degree.

Meanwhile, the traveller lived on berries, nuts and cockroach hearts, a delicacy in great abundance in such a place and full of protein. In the goodness of time the bubbling gently abated and ceased. Above the vat there arose a fragrance of delicate power, a sensation of such promising magnitude, and a newer kind of pungency born of rich natural resource within the vat gathered over time from the sun while the grapes were still on the vine, and from the sweat of the traveller's brow, including the rest of his person. He had at last found what he had been looking for, though previously there had been no rhyme or reason for his restless ways.

And so the traveller ceased his wanderings, put down roots and gathered his energy and his will from the soil for evermore. Other travellers passing by did find a man radiating the warmth of human spirit and great contentment. Many followed suit and took a bath in the hallowed vat before they too put down roots and never roamed again. The vines grew and they *did* roam and spread across the landscape like marching armies making peace. A commune grew and prospered. Some travellers had been women cast out for no sins of their own. Here they found a home and doubly blessed this new domain. Apart from that I know nothing whatsoever about how the Bulgarian wine industry started . . .

FRANCE

D 938

70 LE MANS

2.5   CUON
9   BAUGE

FIRST SIGN THAT WINE IS GROWN AT ALL IN FRAN

CAVE

CAVE A VIN

D62

LA LANDE-CH. 3
MOULIHERNE 10

CAVE
A VIN

ING SOUTH

Ralph STEADman

The Brutal Life History of a Grape

Smashing rocks is big business in the south-west twist of France known as Languedoc-Rousillon, noted for its tough little grapes: Syrah, Grenache, Mourvèdre and Carignan.

The grape is tough because life is tough. It must struggle to survive in the rugged, granite-beaten countryside where it all but died out from the phylloxera scourge at the end of the nineteenth century.

But the superhuman grit of the local people won through, creating a winegrowing area in which the vine, in its struggle to survive, produces a grape whose skins are rich in tannin and charged with aroma and a unique flavour.

The juice is also hard won and draws itself up from nearly two metres down beneath the granite rocks in the sparse subsoil invisible to the outside world.

The Château de Jau has learned to harness this opposition and create for itself a vintage and a pedigree all its own, carefully watched over by the quietly spoken *vigneron* Bernard Daurée, his not-so-quietly spoken wife Sabine and their well-spoken daughter Estelle.

Most of the speaking is about wine and art, and while I cannot pretend to know much about the former, I was given a pretty good crash course, and when it comes to the latter I like to think I can meet them on my own turf.

The Château nestles in the valley at the base of the south-facing slopes of the Corbières overlooking 200 ha (494 acres) of vines planted in rich deep soils. Higher up, however, the slopes ease off on to a plateau, rock solid and volcanic, better suited to bracken, broom, spunkweed and toe spike, beaten grey and sparse with exposure.

But Robert Doutres, a wine aficionado from Perpignan and a family friend, had a fierce dream. If the top metre of granite could be smashed into small pieces and mixed with what little soil there was, plus the granite dust that would inevitably ensue, then Robert was convinced that vines would grow in spite of the brutal nature of their habitat. If the vine suffered to survive, he reasoned, then the struggle would concentrate all its flavours in the fruit, which of course is the

. . . into this prepared ground of broken rocks and minimum topsoil mix is placed the trembling young vinelet to live or die on its own . . .

. . . a mean little brute of a grape emerges, a tough-skinned urchin, small and tight and throbbing with hard-won juices . . .

. . . The vines survive and grow and over years are trained into a seven-branch 'goblet' shape which grows one 'eye' or bunch on each branch. They stand proudly on their own and show it . . .

. . . uncouth hands rip them from their parent with vicious cutting tools . . .

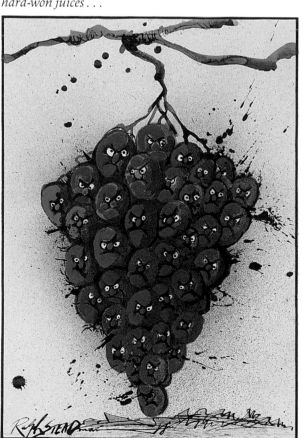

heart of the matter, the 'raisin d'être' as it were. It makes me wonder why my tomatoes never respond to the same treatment. Mine are such greedy little buggers.

The noble grape, however, expects no good life from the severe growing methods of Monsieur Doutres, neither does it get any. It will, though, get his savage devotion, for there is a story about him. Such is his total obsession for the grape and its production from the root to the fruit, the Daurée family feared for the stability of his marriage and insisted that he must, without fail, take his wife to the pictures every Thursday night to re-establish their relationship. They are still married after years of this arrangement, which says a lot about Robert's singlemindedness and perhaps something about his wife too.

So, to continue . . .

. . . the granite is shaken up by a bulldozer then pulverised by a giant crusher. Apparently, if granite is hit right it actually explodes and does all the main work for you, unlike slate which has a tendency to impact in layers and needs to be split along its seams first. . .

. . . into this prepared ground of broken rocks and minimum topsoil mix is placed the trembling young vinelet to live or die on its own (they rarely get talked to, unless they talk to each other). It seems that they survive, for without much ado or much choice, they send their little roots down nearly two metres in search of sustenance and appear to find it. They are forced to burrow through tiny fissures in the submerged solid rocks until they reach the subsoil below. *My* natural reaction would be to go up and flap about in the fresh air. That's why I am not a grape or maybe I was in my last life, and didn't quite make it.

But I digress. The vines survive and grow and over years are trained into a seven-branch 'goblet' shape which grows one 'eye' or bunch on each branch, or they are trained along wires by the 'Guyot' method to resist the high winds of certain sites in this generally inhospitable region. As goblet vines, they stand proudly on their own and show it. . .

. . . a mean little brute of a grape emerges, a tough-skinned urchin, small and tight and throbbing

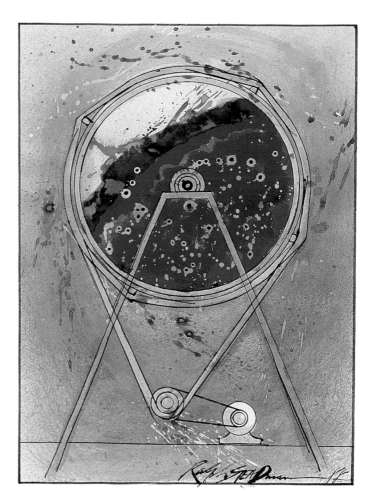

with hard-won juices. For a while, life feels good in the sunshine but anything would after such an unpromising start. It doesn't last long...

... uncouth hands rip them from their parent using whatever cutting tools are available...

... they fly through the air and into a basket alongside, above and below other toughguys of the same sort, crushing and bruising each other as they are carried on the backs of equally tough-looking characters who seem to have grown out of the same soil. These are the *vendangeurs*; they used to be Spanish, but these days, more often than not, are home-grown Frenchmen and women with arms like hydraulic car crushers. This is the grape's rush hour and they have to be transported pretty quickly along bumpy roads to the nearest *cuverie* where the wine is made...

... their suffering is not over yet, because they are tipped unceremoniously into an open channel where an archimedes screw mangles them along into a crusher which squeezes their very flesh to a pulp and extracts their juices down suction pipes...

... or they are tipped into large cylindrical vats, sealed up and turned over and over periodically, until those grapes still oval offer up their contents in a no more civilised manner than the pulverised

lot—though it is believed that the grape responds more favourably to this gentler treatment. They have been macerated instead, and must consider themselves very lucky...

... then they, or it, for now all is a collective juice, is put in the dark, for months, maybe years on

end. The individual souls of these resilient little creatures are now one and they must suffer in torment as they do, at a maintained temperature of 29°–30°C (84°–86°F), occasionally prodded, added to, and 'thieved' to test for specific gravity and tasted for flavour and potency. As time goes by, it, for 'it' it must continue to be now, grows older and perhaps wiser and even philosophic in its dark silent world, united and fermenting to perfection, a stranger to itself. . .

. . . and when it can no longer remember who or why it was, it will be sucked out of itself and through pipes again, coming to a sudden stop inside a glass container, its bottle, separating it yet again from the sum of its other parts. Its world is no longer black, but green, brown or even white. The silence it had become used to is then shattered by the rest of its other parts rattling against its sides in other similar bottles. Like those other parts it will be corked, labelled, controlled and negotiated, then given a name and even a year of birth, though by this time it would not care much anyway. It could only hope that somewhere deep inside its coloured world it may still have a soul. If Robert Doutres' dream is being fulfilled then it certainly would have. . .

. . . when next it breathes the open air it will be poured, scrutinised, sniffed, rotated, criticised or praised, sniffed again, then sucked inside a warm damp opening. Once there it will be allowed to trickle around on moving undulations while mixing involuntarily with other secretions. For a moment, maybe seconds, it will lie still and warm, then quite suddenly, it will be unceremoniously shot forward and downwards by some unseen force, into a silver bucket, and that will be that.

Life must be very puzzling for a grape, and certainly brutal.

Travelling to Bordeaux

On our way to Bordeaux, before we had seen hair or hide of a vineyard, we spent the night in Rouen and as always wandered around the town in the early evening engaged in a pleasurable search for something to eat. We chose L'Etoile d'Or, which turned out to be an Algerian restaurant, a really homely place. I chose Algerian wine, La Mouflon d'Or from the Coteaux de Tlemcen, very soft and very round, like sheep's eyes with square pupils. A woolliness too. Then edgy and rocky, steep and sparse, like its name; a mouflon is a mountain goat. The hint of promise got steeper and sparser yet and it began to taste like dull pewter covered in dust and cobwebs stuck to the roof of my mouth. I considered ordering something else, but that was before the couscous and the merguez sausage and brochette arrived. After that the wine held its own and threw itself at my palate like an impetuous ram followed by an avalanche of falling rocks. The magic mix was, of course, the harmony that follows when food and wine from the same region are served together. Apart they taste a little crude. Together they form a delectable symphony of wild and tasty abandon like peasants at play. It made such a modest little place so memorable.

The rain lashed down between Rouen and Le Mans. It was then that, out of curiosity, I began to think about sighting the very first vineyard as we moved south and approached Saumur, home of some of the finest white wines on the Loire. There wasn't a sign of anything resembling a vine north of Beauge, a classic French town of elongated-high-street charm which sports a twisted tower. It hadn't grown that way. It was made that way. An old man in blue work-denims started noticeably when we arrived, as though life were imminent. Then he hesitated and froze again as he realised we were just slowing down to turn left into the church square. As we turned the corner he fell over, giving him a reason to get up and wait for someone else to turn up and break his day.

The landscape changed. The sight of cows usually means you are nowhere near a vine. Instead we passed strange orchards of what appeared to be seriously trained apple trees, probably Golden Delicious; they displayed wonderful, precise pruning regimented into tight rows and bent into submission for ease of picking by machine. It was fascinating to look at, as with a lot of pristine French agriculture, though reminiscent of a memorial to Kemal Atatürk. The first sight of a Cave de Vin came at Cuon. It looked quaint and closed, so we moved on. Still no vineyard. A few kilometres further on we were in Jumelles and passing the biddiest little vineyard you ever saw, about 100 vines, just about the same size as mine. The place was called Bois de Seronne.

We passed Vivy; seven kilometres (4.3 miles) to Saumur. The countryside was still very Wind in the Willowish, with cows and little streams.

We stayed overnight in Saumur and then moved west on the south side of the Loire, stopping on the way to wander through the damp, clammy atmosphere of an underground mushroom museum, where fungus growths popped out all over the place like an advancing army of alien brains. In the slate-roofed town of Chênehutte on the banks of the Loire we stopped at a small, mean café. Opposite, on the other side of the road, a wino sat slumped with a bottle and a radio playing bad French pop music. He gazed at the radio as if in a trance and I wondered what would happen when the batteries ran out. Had he found it? It looked so new. But his bottle was half-full. Life looked good for a while. The coffee was sparse and grim, like the bar. Austerity and disinfectant squeaked from the place and it was good to get outside.

Here we reached the edge of the Anjou region through Fontevraud. Anjou is best known for its rosé but I never could find a time in the day to drink the stuff. Rosé is in decline and Loire valley wine makers now prefer to make an excellent light red with Cabernet Franc. The larger region around Saumur is best known for its champagne-method sparkling wines stored in vast limestone caves. Chenin Blanc grapes also make excellent semi-sweet still wines.

If you like white wines the Muscadet region of Sèvre-et-Maine is a must. The wines are gentle and rich and we enjoyed a tasting at Domaine de la Grange at Landreau, the property of Pierre and Rémy Luneau. Generally these wines are intended to be consumed young. Their wines have gentle variations of flavour ranging from honey through smoke to pure fruit.

From there we made for Cognac where I noticed a difference in the way the vines were trained. They reminded me of ballet dancers expressing themselves through twisting motions. No two vines move in the same way. Cognac is made from eccentric white grapes which, when distilled, need the wood of the barrel to mature and draw in the rich golden colour of brandy.

A visit to the Eco Musée de Cognac outside the town provided us with an insight into the traditions of the Cognac process. Here we see the bed of the grandfather, the wooden utensils, the fireplace, the old things of the family, the vats and the stills. When it all worked a very old man would sit up all night stoking the fire to keep the liquid at the right temperature, so the spirit steam would rise off and precipitate into another container. He wouldn't dare let the fire go out, otherwise the temperature would drop and arrest the process. He

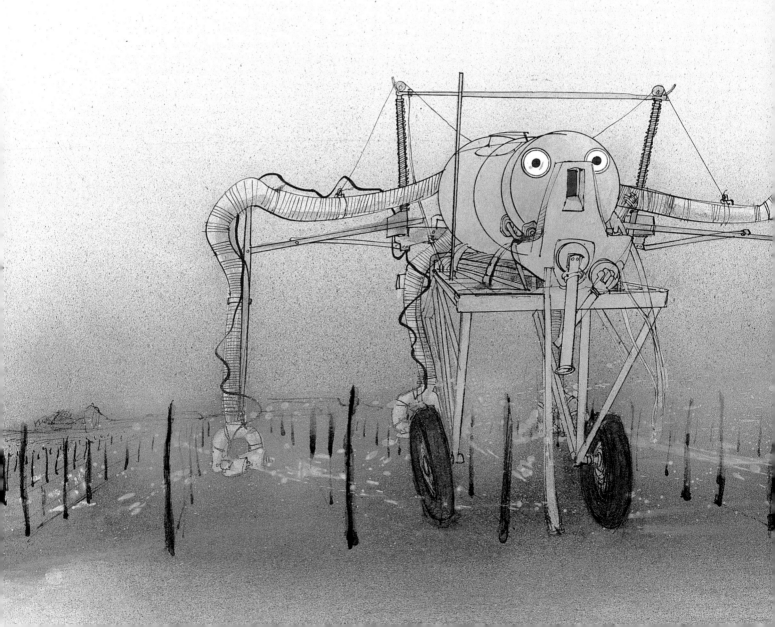

would then do a second distillation, and another very old man would be sent in out of the wilderness to sit on a bench in a black beret and reminisce about the good old days to keep the first old man awake. It was tantamount to murder to fall asleep at a time like this. The process is known as *la surveillance ininterrompue*.

Before Bordeaux and the Médoc there is Blaye and Bourg: the poor man's side of the Gironde. Driving through the region of freshly turned, very chalky, gravelly soil and broken bits of limestone, we stopped at Chateau Peyreyre at St Martin-

Lacaussade, our first tasting. The proprieter, Monsieur Trinque, a very nice gentleman, let us into his hall. He was eating his lunch but was happy to make a possible sale, being a little out of season in April and one of the few caves open for dégustation-vente. He opened a bottle, an '88 Côtes de Blaye, which was rather cold since it had come straight from his cellar. In his carpet slippers he dispensed the wine and we stood sucking and looking at his hat stand. It was a good strong-bodied wine rugged with tannin and fighting the cold like an explorer on his way to the North Pole.

Arriving at St Seurin we got a good view of the estuary between Blaye and Bourg. Situated along the eastern bank of the Gironde, this region was home to wine production long before the Médoc thought of wine. Nothing radical about that, of course; even now, there is a place somewhere in France which lies fallow and will continue to do so until some lucky person finds it, nurtures it and discovers its fine combinations, its strange reverberations and its magical quality of uniqueness. South of here and across the Dordogne and the Garonne, beyond Bordeaux, lies the region of Bordeaux's great whites, the dry Graves, named

Chateau Ausone. St Emilion. April 91

Vineyards of Chateau Moulin St. Georges St Emilion Grand Cru. April 91

after the gravelly soil in which they grow, and the sweet whites of Sauternes where, like some of the Rieslings of the Rhine, the grapes are left on the vine to rot before being picked. These grapes acquire what the French call *pourriture noble* or 'noble rot'.

Also south of here, between the Dordogne and the Garonne, cowers the less noted region known as Entre-Deux-Mers. North of the Dordogne lies illustrious Pomerol and St Emilion, and rustic Fronsac. To me, geographically, this doesn't make sense; it serves to emphasise how difficult it

is to understand the variables which contribute to the mystery of why some regions produce raw material of such quality and others don't. I sometimes wonder what part snobbery, what part artistry, and what part business manipulation play in this game of classification, which sets some apart from others.

Bourg has a rustier, redder soil than Blaye, though there are only 20 kilometres (12.4 miles) between the two. We stopped in Bourg, built on the steep slopes of the Gironde's eastern riverbank. It is a town riddled with crooked streets and

Chateau Saint-

small archways. We bought a couple of bottles of Château La Croix-Davids from a stout gentleman in a silk waistcoat who wouldn't let us taste anything, but said so in the nicest possible way.

We headed back to Blaye to catch the 4.30 p.m. ferry to Lamarque across the Gironde estuary, in the Haut-Médoc region of Bordeaux. Blue-denimed Frenchmen played *boules* among the trees at the quayside. In the adjacent Hotel Café we took a coffee. I lechered after a fabulous old Wurlitzer jukebox, all oranges, yellows and chrome, standing neglected in a corner at a strange and temporary angle. It was far too heavy to carry back to England in a soft-top GTI . . .

We crossed the Gironde, disembarked at Lamarque and headed south to the village of Margaux and Château Rausan-Ségla where we were to be guests for the week.

After a mooch about to get our bearings and settle, we took a short trip to the next village of Cantenac and its cramped supermarket. I looked along the shelves of wine and idly picked up a bottle of Clos Maucaillou Cru Bourgeois Margaux priced at 50 francs. It was an '88 according to the label, until I discovered that someone had changed the numbers from '66 to '88 in biro. What was I to do? Complain? Open it or keep it? Had they run out of '88 labels and used old '66

POMEROL.   April 91.   Ralph STEADman 91.

labels? Had I been swindled, misled, and, more important, had they got any more? I looked up '66 in the wines of Margaux and it is rated an exceptional year along with '45, '70, '75, '85. My God, I thought, perhaps some idiot son had done it. They do have them in these small, interbred French communities. Maybe he had actually gone around his Dad's cellar changing all the '66s to '88s to help him get rid of old stock. I went back to get some more but there was none to be found. The bottle I have lies in my cellar. One of these days I'll pluck up courage, open it and serve it to a real wine buff as a '66.

Having travelled all day we staggered back to the sheer luxury of the château. By seven we were ravenous. We headed north again to Lamarque stopping at every restaurant on the way. Everywhere was full. It wasn't the tourist season but it *was* Saturday night. By the time we reached Lamarque we were moribund. On a Saturday night with nothing but disappointment and a packet of crisps at our disposal, at the centre of the universe of food and drink—moribund is the only word to describe our silent feelings. Quite suddenly, our luck changed. I stopped the car, we dismounted, and like automatons we moved in single file towards an oasis. We had found a place—dark, completely empty, but nevertheless open—the Relais de Médoc. A chef emerged from the depths of a long corridor, and yes! we could eat. All the lights went on. He now had customers. The serviettes were real cloth, and pink. The menus were

richly cossetted in leather vinyl and the prices were horrendously overcooked. It was time to own up. We were not that hungry. It was our mistake. Sorry, M'sieur. The lights went out before we reached the door. 'This is Bordeaux,' he said vehemently, 'not Bolton!' He sounded more disgusted than disappointed.

At last, we found the perfect place, the Café des Sports in Arcins, in the heart of Margaux. It was knockabout, full of people, and it was warm. Tables were laid for a large Saturday-night family gathering, but there was plenty of room for eating, billiards, table football and even ballroom formation dancing, if you fancied it. The proprietor and his wife were delighted to welcome us, but it had to be *bifteck*, salad, chips, and a bottle of

Château Fougey from just around the corner, where it was made and bottled. None better. It was a perfect meal and the Café des Sports became a kind of general base and watering hole when we didn't feel like going too far afield after a day out.

One evening a tasting was arranged at Château Rausan-Ségla with Monsieur Chevalier, the cellar master. We were shown into a small dark room by the main lodge gate. On a long wooden table the bottles had been arranged with six glasses for each bottle. There was the new 1990, an '89 and an '86, for a comparative taste of how the tannin subsides in a typical Margaux as time passes. The blend at Rausan-Ségla, I was informed, is 66 per cent Cabernet Sauvignon, 28 per cent Merlot, 4 per cent Cabernet Franc and 2 per cent Petit Verdot.

Château Margaux

Cabernet Sauvignon is the principle grape variety here and the basis of every successful Margaux vineyard. Merlot adds a warmth of colour and smoothness of body to the wine. The other two grapes are usually the personal choice of the wine-maker, and are added rather like a chef adds herbs and spices to his dishes.

Behind us on the wall was a glass-covered recess with bottles going back to 1845, showing the development of bottle and label. The early bottle glass had a beautiful warm, browny-green colour, very sympathetic, and the labels were gorgeous in their graphic simplicity. The later bottles were a sharper green and the labels coarse by comparison.

The finale came when I was asked to sign the visitors' book on the same spread as a set of Japanese tasters who had been there as guests the week before. I did a flamboyant signature in a blob of red wine from the '86 in the glass I had drawn on the page, then stepped back for the others to sign. I don't quite know why my reflex was so swift but my daughter's friend, Debbie, had a floppy sleeve which was about to smudge my effort and my hand shot out to protect it. A glass of the '86 Rausan-Ségla spread out across the page, since my hand had caught it as I lunged. It swamped the Japanese signatures like the bombing of Pearl Harbour. There was a stunned silence and automatically I was handed a huge roll of tissue to mop up. The page looked fabulous as the wine wash lay naturally with the characters on the page in best Japanese watercolour tradition.

One morning Anna and I decided to make the longish journey to the 'other region of Bordeaux', St Emilion and Pomerol, split awkwardly from the Médoc by the Garonne and the Dordogne, and Entre-Deux-Mers between them. The region is decimated by the arbitrary French planning fiasco of motorways, bypasses, flyovers and mammoth industrial estates wheezing like old athletes whose lungs are long shot by jogging along acrid strips of tarmac. In our own car (part of the problem), it is blessed relief to turn off at an intersection which names the destination of our tentative journey. In the back of my mind I wondered if it was really worth our while to make this trip. As it turned out it was the confirmation of many people's conviction—that St Emilion and Pomerol are the *crème de la crème* of French wine.

The two regions are close, and both feed off one another in legend. They are as different in character as Camembert and Parmesan. St Emilion is full and pastoral, ensconced as a town into a rise and a hollow, swerving lush and full through the vineyards of a day's sunshine. Château Ausone is its crown.

Pomerol is the smallest of the fine winegrowing regions in Bordeaux. Its production is equivalent to 15 per cent of what St Emilion produces, while St Emilion's production is equivalent to 65 per cent of what the Médoc produces. (That sounds quite a lot to me). The vineyards of St Emilion were only classified in 1955, one hundred years after the classification of the vineyards of the Médoc. Pomerol's vineyards have never been classified, but it has within its borders the greatest wine ever which you will never find advertised on any road sign in the region because they never need advertise, and probably don't want to. The wine is known as Château Pétrus. It is made from 95 per cent Merlot grapes which probably accounts for its softness, full fruity flavour, and ability to be drunk young and yet laid down to last forever. In a certain way, it is a pity it is not music which, at least, can be listened to again, with cherished friends. When wine is drunk it is gone, and describing it is not quite the same as enjoying it, or playing it over and over again. It is just too expensive, and I have to record here that, to date, I have not even held a bottle of it in my hands. It's ridiculous. I haven't even tasted it, yet here I am eulogising it like a born-again Christian. It is claimed to be so wonderful that no one dare taste it for fear it might be a disappointment. But those who have tasted it wouldn't dare say what they really think and feel. Château Pétrus is a kind of icon, and every belief needs that.

The region of Pomerol is flat and featureless save for its churches, which are sharp, proud and lapsed Catholic. We did not find the vineyards of Pétrus, nor did we even discover a hint of its presence. Being a romantic, I preferred it that way. That's the stuff of legend and I just hadn't got the time to unveil the truth and that is my best excuse. Instead, we bought a bottle of Lalande-de-Pomerol 1988 from an old lady in her own front room. There were lace curtains on her window, antimacassars on her three-piece suite and cats on every other surface that could be polished. The bottle

Chateau Margaux Approach

lies in my cellar, gathering dust, until I decide to raise it and relive the memories.

Meanwhile, back in the vineyards of the Médoc, the vines are strung like a piano, brilliantly laid out, manicured to perfection, ready for the growing season. All had brand-new stakes and a rose at the end of each row for a practical purpose. A rose will display signs of mildew before a vine does, acting as a timely warning.

Winegrowing workers live in very ordinary boring little box houses surrounded by serious wire fencing creating a compound and it seems that every compound has its crazy, barking dog. The gardens are boring, the walls are cement-faced and their blatant austerity sits like stamped feet in a well-ordered landscape. They look like pieces on a boardgame. In stark contrast, the Châteaux drool with opulence. While Château Margaux itself displays a serene pride in its own supremacy as bearer of the very name of Margaux, Château Palmer, hardly 100 yards away, declares itself in a grander, more flamboyant way, sporting the flags of three nations on its curving tiled roof. The station at Margaux, painted maroon and cream, is pure toy-town. Precise activity in the vineyards was in progress. A machine straddled the rows taking out old vines and putting in new ones using a kind of corkscrew. Little coloured ribbons hold the vines in position on the wires, purples, blues, reds and greens. The whole region is very flat, and you can only detect a slight incline as you move up the Médoc towards St Julien and Château Pichon-Longueville-Lalande in the commune of Pauillac. Château Latour peeps disdainfully at me across the vineyard. This is also the home of Château Mouton-Rothschild and Château Lafite, all first-growth wines. The soil is now very sandy and limestone white as we move into the Haut-Médoc. The landscape rises at this point and you can sense the influence of the Atlantic, particularly in St Estèphe, the home of second-growth wines like Château Cos-d'Estournel, a ridiculous edifice with copper roofs and bells adorning an Arabic-Moroccan-style folly, and Château Montrose.

The entrance to Château Mouton-Rothschild is grand, its drive edged with lines of rounded topiary. It was well-organised to receive coachloads of visitors: its one off-putting feature. Visits by appointment. Baron Philippe de Rothschild took over the family vineyard in 1923 when the Château was rated as a second growth. Its motto was: 'First, I cannot be. Second, I do not deign to be. Mouton, I am.' After struggling for 50 years,

in 1973 his wine was elevated to first-growth status. He replaced the old motto with a new one: 'First, I am. Second, I was. Mouton does not change.'

When you reach the high plateau before St Estèphe you can really feel the breezes from the estuary on the right and the open sea on the left. A small place called Vertheuil sports eleventh- and thirteenth-century churches. Just one kilometre from St Estèphe the soil glows with white chalky gravel and sand from the alluvial drift of the currents at the crown of the peninsula. The clock was striking the hour at five minutes to five as we entered St Estèphe, a cunning device used by workers in the vineyards years ago to warn them that it was about to strike five in just five minutes so that they could be ready to count the exact hour when it arrived.

Nothing was open in St Estèphe, which is the largest of the Médoc appellations, producing over 6,500,000 bottles a year, half of which is consumed in France itself. All the *caves* for *dégustation* were closed except one, Château Pomys, so naturally we stopped for a tasting. Even they were about to close and I sucked and spat with the speed of a submersible pump. It was time to get back to Margaux, stopping on the way to book a table at a restaurant in Tayac, Les Etoiles d'Or. It was run by the noisiest chef I've ever heard, whose strident voice was only matched by the extravagance of his cooking skills. Most of his diners maintained a quiet demeanour as they ate and the chef appeared to be compensating by leaping about the place and shouting joyfully to everyone as though he were trying to fill the restaurant with his *joie de vivre*. We didn't stay long. We were taking off before dawn for the one-day trip up the autoroute and back to Calais. It would be a long day.

The entrance from inside of Château Rausan-Ségla in Margaux where it started.

Jacques Théo, President, Château Rausan-Ségla, Margaux

The 1855 classification of Bordeaux wines will not change. Too much money is involved, too much politics. However good your wine, it will never be as good as a first, second and third growth. You can be better one year. You can be better than Lafite in one year, but not the whole time. When you walk through the vineyards the soil is different from metre to metre. That's why the classifications are as they are. The people making the classifications were taking a lot of precautions, studying the soil itself.

I once spent three months with Matisse on the Côte d'Azur and I was painting with him. I didn't know what I was doing. He was always saying, 'You are so bad, my friend, do something else.' He had the ability to perceive what I could not see myself.

Château Rausan-Ségla

I told Max Schubert, the Australian winemaker, 'You are making good wine'. He wanted to copy wine from Bordeaux or Burgundy. 'You are making a wine which is an Australian wine,' I told him, 'not a German wine, not a Burgundy or a Bordeaux. It does not mean that the wine is bad.'

I was with a so-called expert. I was talking about Beaujolais. He said, 'I'm not talking about that, it's not wine.' Personally, I just stopped talking. It's totally ridiculous. Nothing to do, for sure, with Château Rausan-Ségla, but still it's wine I love. Do you like Van Gogh and do you like Picasso? Personally, I don't like Picasso. I don't understand Picasso. But I don't say that Picasso is a bad painter, which is completely different.

Margaux April 1991.

Château Abel Laurent & parish church · one private chapel of Château La Motte. MARGAUX.

We are in the same vicinity as Château Margaux. We are even in the same vineyard. We are in the same climate. It is normal to try to be as good as them. But we are different.

In June, when the grapes are already formed, you can see how many you have on each bunch. If you find you have too many grapes you just cut. You've got to get the sugar. You've got to get everything into a certain number of grapes.

Ralph: I could tell the difference between the '89 and '90. The '90 was very big.

Théo: Perhaps the biggest of the century.

Nicolas Joly, la Coulée de Serrant, Savennières

If you talk about an appellation it is the soil in one spot but if it is just a dead support and the growth only comes from what you introduce from outside there is no point in having an appellation. Soil is alive. If you use weedkiller that life is dead after seven years. To grow you need an outside support, a supply of chemicals. We have never been so close to starving conditions because people are so dependent on artificial support.

Postscript
1988 Château Pomys, Cru Bourgeois, St Estèphe

March 24th, 1992. It was time to drink this wine, a roadside bottle I had bought from the only place open during our visit to St Estèphe. It was bought in haste and bought to regret, though I didn't expect a Cru Classé because it wasn't pretending to be one.

Bordeaux is the same as everywhere else: if you want to find something really good locally, don't buy souvenirs. Without, I hope, sounding too derogatory, all the châteaux now in such a legendary region entice the passing traveller with a kind of designer plonk for those who, like myself, believe in everything they are paying for if the label looks convincing. If it is from a place of proven pedigree, you convince yourself, with the help of your new half-baked knowledge, that it has to be good. There is an all-too-common marketing ploy at work in even the best of regions these days which uses this technique of selling off an inferior product in spiffy packaging and charging twice as much as it is worth. It's a game and it seems to have been endorsed as quite legitimate, because it's business. I don't think reputable places are doing themselves a favour by employing this kind of marketing, though I realise it's a survival mechanism for unloading a lesser wine for a large profit.

Travellers often stop the car with a 'leave this to me, honey' look on their faces. The place is set up to take your money. There is a lot of wood about, take-away boxes with burned-in traditional lettering, dark dank corners, gold-embossed labels and shiny laminated brochures to confirm the wisdom of your choice. There are even cheese biscuits to clean your palate. After all, we are experts here and we stick together. Generosity is rife. The prices don't even bother us. The seduction is on. It must be good wine. There is no rubbish in the Médoc. Goodness me, no, that's why we're here, to savour the best. Buying is investing. *This* is to lay down. What would *you* do if you had a rich and abundant product on your hands and you had to shift it to make way for next year's waterfall? Great lakes have somehow to be unloaded in the best possible taste. It's an annual problem. Nature is relentless, even in today's stressed environment.

Passing motorists will believe anything. It seems natural, gentrified and accessible. We become a dumping ground for the rejects of the best châteaux. The wine can be good but it can also be rubbish. The vats must be emptied. The best bet for them is to 'sell it down' to be bottled

The First Little Vineyard of Bois de Serronne

Chateau de JAU — EARLY MORNING — Ralph STEADman H

and labelled and put in a roadside shop with all the dripping sweat of ancient bullshit hanging from a stone arched ceiling as a price tag. Otherwise, it's the supermarket, el cheapo. Well, we fall for it every time. I did and I do. I'm a sucker for crafted peasant elegance, but these days I try to resist, even though I feel I may be missing out. Who knows? You may be passing up the chance to buy the overflow at knock-down prices from a particularly generous harvest of a budding Lafite.

If you are in doubt and it is spoiling your holiday, go and buy something you fancy from a supermarket in the region and say you bought it from some colourful proprietor who sported huge nose hairs and had dead pheasants hanging from his belt. Your friends will believe anything.

As regards the wine I bought, it made me think of rusty arrowheads launched at point-blank range into my solar plexus. You win some; you lose some. Never again—until the next time.

Nicolas Joly, la Coulée de Serrant, Savennières

If you decide to change the barrels every 20 years you take the best possible oak. This is absolutely normal and it doesn't affect the wine and marries with it. But from that position going to the one where you change your barrels every year, it is a sure way to demonstrate that the wine is not strong enough on its own.

If you start to add things to your wine—nobody will tell you this—to make it more caramel, to make it more yellow, to give a little taste of violet on the palate because the wine is supposed to have a violet taste, that clearly proves the point that the wine itself cannot properly achieve its intention. These are technical wines. They will have absolutely no capacity for ageing.

They don't even know what names to give their wines. They are trying to make a little story and why is that? Because the soil is not expressing itself in the fruit.

Tell me where in France we are not using chemicals. There is no place. Everywhere is affected the same way.

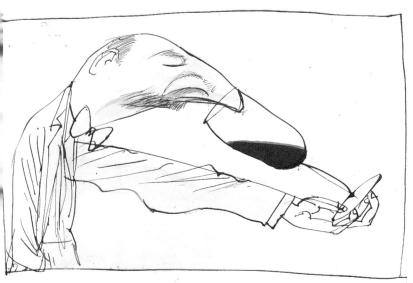

France: October 1987

Seeking a guide to wines that I could trust, or at least a guide to my own palate, I decided to keep notes of bottles of wine I encountered on my journey through France. God willing, it was to be an ongoing experience which would eventually grow into a useful list, at least for my own benefit if not for others.

Realising that sometimes even a wine generally acknowledged as good can taste as poor and indifferent as any other if the mood is not right, if the food is not right and the ambience less than could be desired, I decided that a wine should be spoken about in relation to its environment and what is happening in its immediate vicinity. This would be as good a guide as any from the experts—hence the very personal notes. Times and places are as much the expression of enjoyment as the wine itself.

October 13th 1987
We were thirsty after several hours of travel and abstinence and came at last to a small hotel called the Hostellerie des Tilleuls. After freshening up and changing for the evening, the anticipation of what one is going to eat and drink is always at its most intense and, if one can manage to resist aperitifs, the pleasure at the first sip of a good wine is at its highest. So I chose a wine at random, a Bordeaux, called Château Grand Chemin, Côtes de Bourg 1983 and asked for immediate delivery while we perused the menu: Sauté de Sanglier Desosse, Salade Buissonnière de Saumon et Flétan Fumés, Pièce de Canette aux Raisins Frais—140 francs. I'll take it.

The wine arrived. A light taste—a thin wine that slipped easily between tight cold lips parched by time and travel. The night outside was cool and autumnal. The wine's bouquet thickened with bread on the palate.

We finished it with the Plateau de Fromages. The real fruit of the wine tumbled out and shimmered its way down my throat into a cave of contentment. A palate freshener of genuine lemon jelly and lemon juice with a hint of vanilla followed.

There seemed to be a tragic lack of people—where was everybody? Perhaps it was the clinical double-glazing destroying the ambience of an old French family house.

All the things they try to get into Nouvelle Cuisine were there but with wholesome plenty—it was the best meal ever to Anna—who remembers the best?—delicate yet generous, enough for the hungriest and maybe the greediest.

October 14th 1987
Le Parrot. Rue Parrot, Paris 12. Bourgogne Aligoté. Everyone drinks this modest little wine in Le Parrot near the Gare du Lyon—it drives on the right tracks down the palate but from the wrong platform. Mis en bouteille by Ropiteau Frères.

1982 Savigny les Beaune. An unexpected metal aroma but, after melon, it darkens and rides over the palate like fifteen horses, holding its own in spite of the fruit. And then after the prosciutto it released its hold on itself and drove all my resistance into a gorgeous corner of the table where I remained hoping for a second bottle. After the rabbit cooked in cider, I sucked on the tablecloth and my host's wife's napkin. *Cela m'est égal.* But

then as if this were not enough, as I smoked a cigarette (I roll my own, any slob does), my host produced the ace, a 1975 Monthelie Premier Cru Clos des Champs.

The smell, the aroma, the attack hit both nostrils simultaneously and spread then to the extremities of my face. My eyes watered like melons and drew back their liquid to balance the sheer glow of reality this wine offered. Each wine at each stage of every meal is as different as the rest but if given at the right moment cauterises the resistance and leaves only the pleasure. A morsel of Camembert blew my tongue through the roof of my mouth and I was replete. No, sated. A touch of chèvre (goat's milk cheese) and I desperately wanted to swallow my tongue which possessed the total experience.

October 15th 1987

We went for lunch to an old favourite of ours: Chez Georges, a French-Russian restaurant in Rue Mazarine in the 6th arrondissement. We had been walking all morning from the 12th to the Hôtel de Ville, and then round the whole of the Musée d'Orsay: 4 hours, leaving me with legs of jelly and pains on my flexing calves. We were greeted by the Maître Georges, the Russian proprieter, like old friends and we *were* old friends. Une bouteille du vin rouge immédiatement—no aperitif—and black bread. Posters covered the walls, posters of

exhibitions of painters. Such painters as Jacques Barrère, Dallos, Andrea Vizzini, Gaby Edrei, Pierre Risch at the Galerie André Candillier, Gérard Diaz, Michaus and of course Cremonini and Lapicque—all completely unknown. Where else in the world do restaurants advertise each and every expo of even the humblest painter? A true sign of a civilised culture. I love them for it.

The wine arrived: Bourgueil from the Domaine des Raquières, made by P. Maître et R. Viémont.

I tried desperately to savour the first taste on my tongue, but thirst got the better of me and I gulped a mouthful which burst inside me like a warm sensuous bomb. I followed it with a piece of black bread and thought only of France and the sheer joy of booze at the right moment. Its bouquet was warm and gentle, without a hint of harshness on the palate and with a seductive rounded flavour.

I waited for the Blini with Salmon which I knew would screw the palate, but I was determined to see how the wine stood up to it. Red wine with salmon is sacrilege but it also has its rebellious advantages which a puritan would never understand. It worked: salmon, cream, melted butter, squeezed lemon and Bourgueil—only a glutton and a slob can really know how wonderful that is, filled as I was with anticipation for the main course of Chicken Kiev cooked by real Russians. The wine had restrained itself and now took its place in the grand order of things, a genuine

trooper which gave as good as it got.

By the time the Kiev arrived there were about two large mouthfuls of rich redness left in the sharp olive-green bottle. The Kiev arrived with a sparse helping of carrot and kohlrabi and brown macrobiotic barley and a thin butter sauce.

Kerpow! Bang! Whang! Donk! Shazam! Whack! The complete explosion erupted, burst out to fill my whole system with a true gourmet's delight—a fullness with a bloated inability to move. In France, the effect is usually like that—which is what makes them the masters. They know the combinations, especially those Russians who domicile here. Always well worth a try if you

happen across such an establishment. I looked at Anna and she looked at me and we both knew how the other felt. Never again.

Don't be silly, that was just the joke at the end of the meal. But wait, there's the shot of ice-cold vodka with the coffee—that, for the true gorging connoisseur, is *the* moment. (Incidentally, the moment de la moment for Anna would be if she could only do her No. 2. Hasn't been since Monday and now it's Thursday, so you can imagine!!)

A couple of Alka Seltzers for me and I'm as right as rain.

That evening, we go to La Connivence, in the 12th. I decided on *l'inspiration du jour*—the jugged

hare. Anna and my publisher were going to try the tuna. The patron tries hard to find a perfect wine to suit both fish and meat.

Anna tries the aromas: the wine smells of raspberry jelly. The first hit of the aroma for me was furniture polish—perfect. Not too important. Good for two bottles so that one can work well afterwards without falling asleep.

It's called Château du Breuil 1986—an Anjou Rouge. Not the best wine but very drinkable. The *patron* cut the grapes, owns the château and makes the wine. An excellent start for a debutant.

The restaurant was filled with characters of a most varied and eccentric nature, all enclosed by their own arc-shaped brick wall, one brick thick.

Oh my God, the man who owns the next flat to ours has arrived, complete with an entourage of eight or ten people. He's wearing a yellow sleeveless pullover: a genuine turn-off. They sit at an adjacent table—but don't look now. Yet they do, one at a time. Our neighbour has told them that they are our neighbours—we are all neighbours

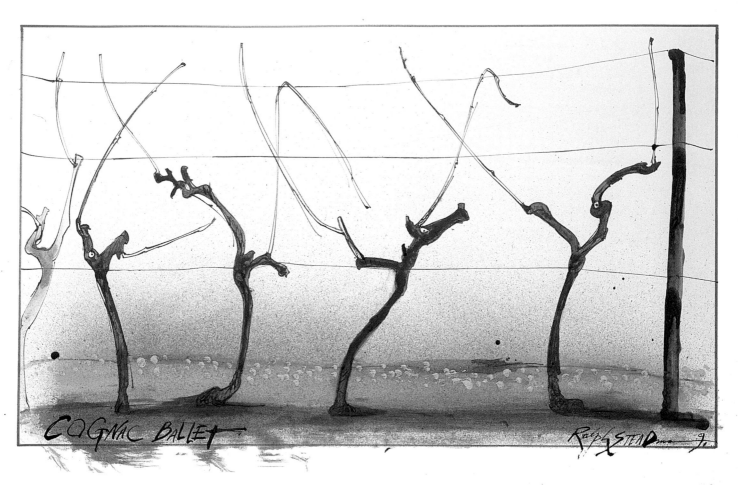

COGNAC BALLET

Ralph STEADman

together. Keep your distance, otherwise we could end up in the most ghastly singsong—French songs too!

How much for a parking space? Never mind the wine, we want somewhere to park our car, and the back of our place is going for 50,000 francs per

space. It's a steal when you realise that down the road the French government is building the newest, biggest opera house. Just down the road— would you believe it?

The wine? Oh, the wine, well, I'll keep the half bottle we didn't drink and put it in my car radiator.

October 16th 1987

Côtes du Lubéron (Tête de Cuvée) 1986 from the Cellier de Marrendon at La Tour d'Aigues lay uncomfortably on my palate. We had waited for service at least 15 minutes in the Au Limonaire on the Rue de Charenton in the 12th, and inside the 15 minutes we had decided to change to something else. You can't deal with the inferior too seriously in France. Using a serviette I tried some on my shoes and the leather responded with a shine.

The next bottle was a Côtes du Rhône 1985 from the Enclave des Papes. Slightly watery but nevertheless acceptable enough to compliment the Rôti de Porc with Purée d'Oignon and Potatoes. An average meal which fills the stomach but does nothing to nourish the spirit. It didn't help that I kept hitting the back of my head on the corner of a chipboard construction which probably covered faulty French wiring insulated only by its own greasy dust of ages. All part of the atmosphere. This sharp repeated knock certainly did nothing to help the bouquet of the wine, struggling to get through to my brain. Only the pain got through. All my life I will remember these two wines, if only for the sharpness of the chipboard corner. The restaurant is also on a corner. The waitress was a little less sharp—even vague, but sympathetic. I was afraid that she might bring me the dirty glasses on the bar instead of my Rôti de Porc.

That evening we go to Gaspard de la Nuit. The wine we choose is a bit sharp, but not unpleasant: wild horses restrained by chains. It is Château Vieux Moulin 1982, a Bordeaux Supérieur. That's what they say, but don't be fooled, just believe a little.

We need bread but they always forget, like every restaurant. It is such a simple device, but they always forget. What about our palate? It is so delicate, so sensitive. Never mind. We now have

Vapor methd.

Ralph STEADman

UNE SURVEILLANCE ININTERROMPUE

the vocabulary to judge and imagine the bread.

Here at the Gaspard de la Nuit even the menu is wine-coloured. 'Est-ce que vous avez du pain?' There you are—the whole place erupts into a cauldron of activity as they search, no, reach out for the nearest basket of bread. Curtains are maroon-velvet-buff-come-cigarette smoke, with dark vinyl upholstery. The first course, Terrine de Legumes, was a magnificent jelly-covered assortment of vegetables, with a pure taste, light and wholesome, with a garlic-mayonnaise sauce flavoured with mustard and tarragon. The herb exploded in my mouth with the warmth and dimensions of something more superior, yet this average little wine was giving me the same experience without the pain of price. Hold back before you taste, even though I myself dive straight in—hold back and reflect, prepare your palate for the flavour that comes with the juices that only good food can provide and the ambience which allows the body to respond with sympathy.

There are paintings on the wall. If you know Vlamminck, you will see that this place likes him but cannot afford the real thing. The man on the next table has almost as much hair as me but he does not possess much personality. Nevertheless he is trying and his voice has an acrylic resonance—can you imagine it? He speaks like Scarpia, the chief of police and principal villain in Tosca singing on a bad night—and he speaks more than anyone else on the table.

The wine, by the way, is fine! Not only fine but rising to the challenge—to the palate—wresting from the depths all the aspirations of a younger self. And there are letters on the bottle. The wine looks important. Beware the letters on the bottle but don't despise them.

They are not enjoying themselves on the next table. But never mind, they chose, and in their way they make the best of a bad job. Imagine duck surrounded by pears, all pointing inwards and cooked to perfection. It's delicious and the remnants of the bottle of Château Vieux Moulin disappears in a wealth of taste and seduction.

October 17th 1987
At Meudon, Bellevue, the house of my publisher, looking down over Paris. I stirred and shot my palate through with a large Famous Grouse before enticing my responses with a Bordeaux of exceptional pedigree: 1982 Château la Chapelle Haute-Roque, put in bottles by a complete stranger who must have understood the moment of internment. The home of our friend and publisher lies on the

side of a hill. The wine slips down my slope with ease. One feels the house sigh and nestle into the hillside. Some things are right, and the wine enters centre stage—the spirit of the atmosphere which comes to visit at exactly the same time as we do. Saliva-inducing knicknacks of curried samosas are served up as an appetizer and the wine keeps sliding. Then rice, caked and light, with Poulet Rôti. When the Roquefort arrived and was tasted, the house slipped down the hill a little further. The view was even greater and more extensive.

October 18th 1987
The jazz-and-blues evening at Au Limonaire. We had arrived at 8:05, the first course arrived at 8:40. We were in no hurry. I had, as it happened, chosen the Terrine de Poisson—not a dead ringer for a red wine, but I was still choosing reds as a matter of course. In spite of the invasion of my finely tuned palate by this fish terrine, the St Joseph 1985 from the Caves Bessac roamed home with the certainty of a true vintage wine. 1985 was indeed a fine year for this region.

The fish was immaterial. The lovely girl by my side made all the difference—a complete stranger but I felt I had known her all my life. A tranche of bread, and the fish was no longer a problem. The wine was a masterpiece. Beneath the arches there dwelt a ravenous troll whose satisfaction was my only concern. I am an inverterate wine drinker who can, if pressed, drink enough for a restaurant of clients and still rise the next day to face it like a trooper.

This was no ordinary night. We were here for food, wine, jazz and blues and we would take it in that order. How did we get here? Well, knowing this person and that in our *quartier* we had begun to seek the real life. What is contained in a bottle of wine is certainly more than the wine, no matter how good it is. I love the stuff, but it takes more than loneliness and a cavern of solitude to bring it alive, and we were surrounded by young people full of anticipation who delight in the cheapest stuff the house had to offer. They were here for the complete experience: food, cheap wine and music. A perfect combination which gives to the most rakish brew a bouquet of rare distinction. A fact overlooked by the connoisseur.

We happened to be sitting in this place waiting more than eating, drinking and enjoying because we are still paying for the night before—which was, by my standards, a night of the long liqueurs: knives with their own special brand of violence.

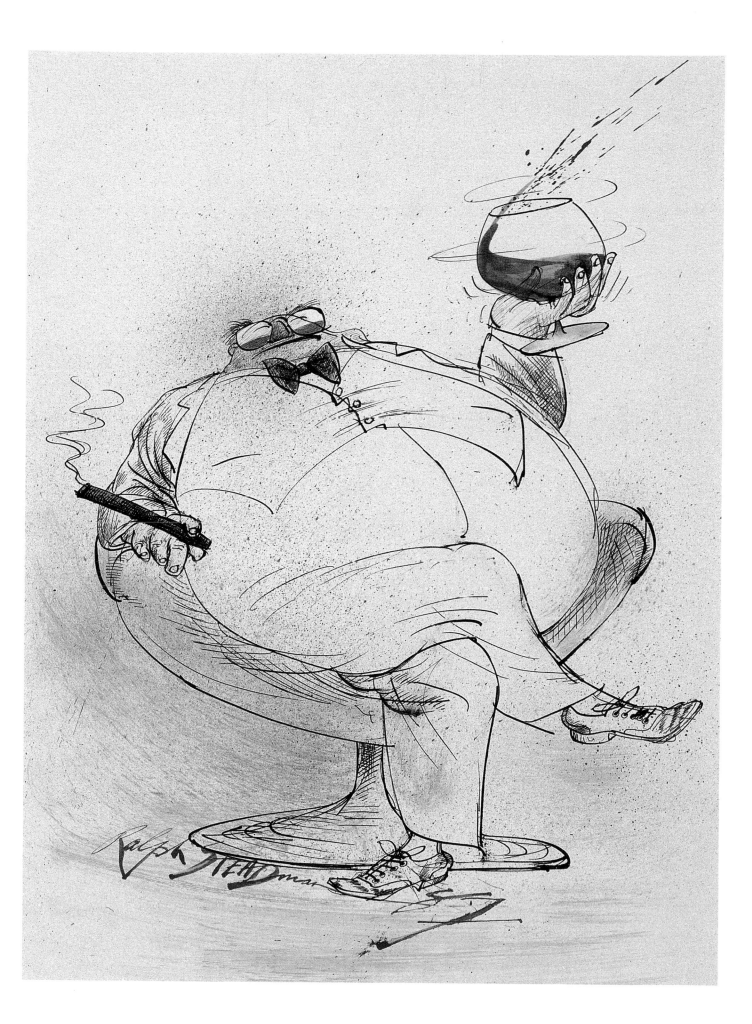

Oh, my God – I've forgotten to do Champagne.

1855 — and all that

Pierre Gnignancourt shuddered and pulled up the high fur collar of his Girault de Pranguy Astra-khan coat. As he left the Boulevard St Raspail and turned on to the river front at Quai d'Orsay the wind cut at his over-shaved chin and ripped it as raw as the streets he walked on.

'Mon Dieu,' he muttered to himself, 'I wish I 'ad left my beard on. Damn women! She would have got used to eet if I 'ad persisted.'

He sought refuge in the Café Estaminet and downed a cognac and café like a hungry waif. 'Am I really a part of thees? Why me? All I know ees that grapes grow and eet make wine. Ask any peasant and 'e will tell you the same.' He pulled out his watch from the silk fob beneath his coat and checked the time. 'I 'ave time for one more.' He relaxed as the spirit rolled down his throat and burst inside him.

Pulling his coat about him again he made for the door. A blast of cold air swept into the café as it opened, provoking comment from the seated habitués huddled over their own particular comfort. 'Hey! Give us your coat or buy us a drink,' they grumbled as the door closed behind him, but he was far too preoccupied by the task that lay ahead to notice.

His tongue still felt like an old saddle that had been left gathering white fungus in a ditch.

'How can I judge the nuances, the finest and the best? I, a cripple in retreat, with an army set against me?'

He leaned over the edge of the stone barricade which overlooked the Seine and gazed at the heaving scum of a city's daily refuse. He looked into the browny-green darkness like a witch hoping for a miracle in her looking glass.

'Mon Dieu! Do I really look like that? Can such a blasphemous eruption like me have such responsibility?'

He crossed the Pont des Invalides and turned right on to the Cours La Reine on the right bank and caught sight of Auguste Diderot, the lawyer, and an old friend. He too was making his way to the same destination, the Annexe des Beaux Arts, at the end of the Avenue Montaigne, recently constructed to house the Palais de l'Industrie. This edifice was the pride of La Première Exposition Universelle de Paris, built to impress the world and overshadow the Great Exhibition of 1851, held four years earlier in England. The might of Empire demands these huge displays of pride and achievement, and nothing was too grand for such an occasion. The French anyway had been holding such international exhibitions since the late eighteenth century; they were far superior to the more local bazaar-like affairs conducted by the English until Albert's show stopper of 1851.

The two friends greeted one another and continued towards the monstrous facade. The portico loomed ahead of them, a vast semi-circular headed doorway above which towered a carved stone figure of a woman wearing a spiked crown and a hugging diaphanous slip, a goddess representing the spirit of the new age. She pulsated confidence and looked like living flesh.

Pierre and Auguste were waived on through the great barrier leading into the magnificent hall, while the general public bustled impatiently in a disorderly manner, trying to buy their tickets. Queuing was unknown to the French and anyway completely illogical to the French mind.

'They'll need Napoleon's civil guard to sort out a rabble like that,' muttered Auguste. 'They are late today.'

Pierre and Auguste passed by the Prussian stand dripping marble fire surrounds, fountains oozing ornamentation like molten volcanic rock, the new-style gas wall-lamps hanging limp and groaning under the perilous weight of encrusted castings. Startling plumes for military headgear poured themselves out of crafted metalwork like gossamer. Water spewed upwards from the beak of an upturned swan, whose neck was supported by a figleaved youth sheltering his head with his other hand from the falling cascade. This item had been kindly loaned by the King of Prussia from the gardens of his residence in Charlottenburg.

On past the English exhibits, they went, the carved drawing-room pianos by Messrs Collard and Collard of London, a state bedspread of exquisite needlework worked entirely by English-women draped over coiling asps of deep mahogany enshrining a fanciful depiction, in wood, of Boadicea surrounded by beckoning angels and cherubs, reaffirming the right of the English to rule the world. 'To be conceived in such a bed would thrust greatness upon the simplest mortal,' remarked Pierre with a lascivious smile.

A vase, representing science, the industrial arts, astronomy, philosophy, mechanics and poetry, in the guise of Newton, Bacon, Shakespeare and Watt, stood before them on a pedestal. Between each figure oozed naked bodies displaying the practical operations of science and art. War, rebel-

Exposition Universelle
Jardin du Palais
de
L'Industrie
PARIS
1855

Ralph STEADman 1855

lion, hatred and revenge were depicted, over-thrown, helpless and in chains. The only books on display were hidebound impossible tomes entombed in bookcases built like prison walls.

Their walk through the great nave of the exhibition was relieved momentarily by the Spanish stand which displayed exquisitely crafted guitars constructed by Don José Gallegos from Málaga. His son Pablo played one of the instruments as his proud father beamed at the passing visitors.

The French stands were lighter, florid and sensuously adorned by voluptuous nudes and sensitive landscapes by Jean-Baptiste Corot with two or three views by him of Paris in the 1830s. Unctuous representations of nature's idyll dripped like treacle from the paintings of Bougereaux and Fragonard, reminding the visitor that the aesthetic spirit was not forgotten, in France at least, by this new-age industry.

Daguerreotypes, the magical new photographic technique perfected by Louis Daguerre and Nicéphore Niepce, were proudly displayed along with the mysterious *chambre noire* used by them to obtain these intriguing images. Porcelain clocks in vase-like forms flanked by cherubs stood like ornate robots and ticked resolutely. They were just striking noon as Pierre and Auguste arrived at the tree-lined trellises decorating the landscaped gardens of the Palais de l'Industrie incorporated within the massive nave.

Ten dignified gentlemen were already gathered beneath a handsome mulberry tree adorning the trellised courtyard. They stood around a series of casks which served as a support for a table top, which in turn supported groups of dark bottles, each containing wine from the most important regions of France. These men were the elite group of wine experts, lawyers, bankers, merchants, courtiers and négociants who were all, in one capacity or another, involved with wine. Pierre and Auguste made up the twelve members of this panel of wine tasters who had gathered to establish once and for all the finest winemaking region in France. Prices realised over the last one hundred years became an initial guide to determine the superiority of some wines over others. On this meeting depended the standard of excellence that was to be upheld as a quality benchmark to govern the making of wine henceforth.

'Ah, Pierre! I didn't recognise you. You must 'ave a new mistress. You 'ave cut off your beard.' It was Patrice Debuisson-Fluckingeux, Directeur of the Institut du Vin, who spoke. He always held centre stage at the wine-tasting ceremonies. He

was telling the story of Jacques Pouderoux, another member who had been discovered along the Quai de Conti trying to make love to an empty bottle of Château Tronquoy-Lalande at 4 a.m. dressed only in a nightshirt and a Jacobite hat.

'You are right, Patrice,' said Pierre, 'she is so fussy, but oh, such a darling. She make me crazy. I would do anything for 'er.'

'Be careful, Pierre, she does not persuade you to cut everything else off in your enthusiasm to please 'er. Ze same 'appened to Gérard de Montgolfier. 'e cut off everything, for 'is little Roxanne, n'est-ce-pas, Gérard?'

Gérard, who was reaching for a ripe mulberry before it fell, nodded, and popped the soft sweet fruit between his puffy lips.

'But Gérard was clever. 'e kept 'is nose. Gérard's nose ees second to none. 'e use it for everytheeng. Et toi, Auguste, 'ow ees Madame Diderot? Still making zose gorgeous leetle pâtés from zee boules of bulls? She remind me of Madame Defarge, always waiting for somezink to drop into 'er lap.'

'My wife ees very well and she sends 'er regards,' replied Auguste.

'She keeps 'er love for you, eh, Auguste? Heh, heh, heh, heh!'

Bernard Frizot, the Secretary, interrupted and said, 'Gentlemen, I theenk we should taste ze wine.'

'Bonne idée,' replied Roland Bonnemaison, Treasurer of the gathered Institut.

Patrice Debuisson-Fluckingeux drew up his substantial frame with his podgy hands and addressed his colleagues. 'What we 'ave 'ere, gentlemen, is ze very best of ze very best. Eet ees up to you to establish what wine we can declare the Grand Premier Superior Formidable Incroyable Cru.'

A waiter stepped forward dressed immaculately in black with a huge white apron down to his ankles and began to pour from one of the bottles opened previously to allow the wines to catch their breath before tasting.

'Ze first bottle we shall taste ees from Château d'Yquem. It ees a Bordeaux Blanc, from Sauternes. Considered a dessert wine we offer it to you wiz an appetizer of foie gras.' A Noblesse de Robe, Comte Alexandre de Boudoux Guestier offered the glasses around.

'Nice bottle,' remarked little Freddy Dressen, always at a loss for something to say.

'You are right. It ees a bottle made for a prince, crafted in ze famous blue glass of Nantes. Ze wine ees ze finest ever tasted, but gentlemen, don't take my word for it. I only make zis wine.'

Everybody nodded and furtively looked at each other before sipping and spitting into a sawdust-filled bowl. This was followed by a Château Suduiraut, another of the Comte's offerings, and a Château Sigalas-Rabaud from a friend of his, Henri Doublet. Several others were offered in quick succession, Coutet, Climens, La Tour Blanche, Guiraud and Rieussec. Lots of spitting and viewing of colour against the light, twisting of goblets and sounds of approval ensued and everyone generally agreed that Château d'Yquem was the winner by a nose for the Comte Alexandre de Boudoux Guestier who proudly thanked everyone for the honour.

At last the white wines were moved aside and fresh bottles already opened were brought to the table and dispensed by the waiter into clean goblets. Dried biscuits were offered to clean the palate and the red-wine classification began in earnest. The members of the committee looked into the rich red colour in their glasses like fortune tellers peering into a crystal ball. Monsieur Gallant-Dooley, a négociant from Pauillac, spun his glass effortlessly and everybody followed suit, watching the tears of wine slide down their glasses, weeping like neglected children.

The wine was a Château Lafite-Rothschild and its sales had rockcted in recent years according to Monsieur Gallant-Dooley. Roger Rabaud-Promis des Granges held his nose over the liquorous aromas euphungulating above the rim, and the rest sniffed in varying degrees of intensity and flamboyance in their attempts to display a practised élan. Maurice Doubourdieu had a particularly long and sharp nose and his enthusiasm left him with a red dew drop hanging from its tip.

'I like zis wine,' he declared, 'Eet 'as body, eet 'as complexity, eet 'as strength, eet 'as structure and eet 'as a shape like no other.'

'A shape?'

'Oui, a shape, eet remind me of a wedding cake.'

'What kind of wedding cake?'

'My wedding cake,' says Doubourdieu.

'But you are not married, Monsieur.'

'You do not 'ave to be married to 'ave a wedding cake!'

'You have a wedding cake?'

'I 'ave designed a wedding cake. But, alas, it ees not yet made. Eet 'as pillars and different layers getting smaller as zey reach ze top. Ze lady I wish to marry ees promised to another.'

'Ees there any more of zis? Eet ees quite sharp and tannic.'

'Aha, now there ees a statement, sharp and tannic,' repeated the Comte, 'you are right. Eet ees a young wine for such a strength. Can you be more specific?'

'Mais oui, very sharp and very tannic. Like—er—icebergs.'

'Like icebergs? Interesting. Who says icebergs?'

'I like ze bottle,' said little Freddy Dressen again, still unable to think of anything to say.

'What 'as zat got to do wiz icebergs?'

'Freddy ees right,' interrupted Diderot, 'when you 'old ze bottle up to ze light you can imagine the North Pole.'

'More like Greenland to me,' suggested Maurice Doubourdieu, whose sharp nose was now like a blood-soaked arrow head.

There was much muttering about Greenland and one committee member, Jacques Collombert-Dayonberthier, had actually been to Greenland for a youthful wager and had difficulty holding his glass due to the results of severe frostbite. He disagreed and thought the light shining through the bottle was the atmosphere in Les Halles in the eye of a trout on the slab of a fishmonger.

'Impossible,' protested the Comte, 'Zis wine would be insulted to be drunk wiz a fish. But now, gentlemen,' he continued, 'ze Château Latour, also from Pauillac, a legendary drink of great depth and a classic Cabernet nose. Well, gentlemen, what do you think?'

'Mmmmmm,' chorused everyone, sucking air through their pursed lips like gargling wind passing through the pipes of the organ in the Notre Dame the day rain leaked through the roof.

Little Freddy Dressen, who never could get the hang of sucking, choked on the intense concentration of fruit and tannin and scattered red wine over the assembled throng.

'Freddy, you clumsy fool, my cravat is ruined. Eet will never come out.' The Comte wore a particularly spectacular white silk cravat.

At last Freddy thought of something to say. 'Salt,' he declared.

'Salt? What salt?'

'Eet is a remedy from ze Madame Beeton Cookbook. She spill many things and she has a remedy for everytheeng. She can get potage out of your pants and beetroot out of your tablecloth. She even know how to make rhubarb wine, and wine from tea, and rose petals, orange peels and petit pois. I 'ave a bottle of 'er favourite 'ere in my pocket. Eet ees called ze Turnip Wine. Per'aps after zer Margaux we should like all to 'ave a leetle taste?'

body, short legs and a suctorial form of mouth. The antennae were filiform and obtuse.'

Mr Fitch noted that the insects were invariably females, and the eggs produced by each numbered several thousand (bloody women!). The eggs turned to larvae, which ascended to the upper part of the vines. Each larva in its turn, by biting or eroding the plant surfaces, produced a new gall, which speedily became enclosed in the same manner as the parent. The reason, it was discovered later, why the insects which dwelled on the plant were all females was because identical insects were noted but they possessed wings and did not therefore hang about. They were reckoned to be the males. As it turned out both males and females have wings and once established spread their offspring at a fearful rate—one of nature's most prolific examples of flying sex.

Those which did hang about, however, in the course of development modified themselves to become the root-inhabiting variety.

Mr Fitch ascertained that the malformations produced on the vines did no apparent damage, at least not to American vines.

But in Europe it was a different story. Under hothouse conditions at Kew, the roots of apparently clean vines were also examined and found to harbour a subterranean grublike creature which sucked away the fluids of the plants. These findings were not published until 1869, by which time vineyards on both sides of the lower Rhône and other regions, including the Alps, were deeply affected.

Peasants familiarly referred to the disease as 'le blanquet' or 'rot', but phylloxera was to prove far worse than they imagined. It caused a kind of gangrene or decay of the vine roots, the gangrenous matter having a blackish colour.

Various drastic methods were employed to halt the growing menace, and poisonous solutions such as ammonia, hydrogen sulphide, carbolic acid and even arsenic were tried—but the little buggers kept on going.

The plague appeared to 'march like an army'. Although the disease was first called *Rhizaphis* by Professor Planchon from Montpellier University, a name which means 'root aphid', the search was on for a winged insect which would account for the speed with which the scourge spread. Planchon eventually found one in the chrysalis state. It resembled a tiny yet elegant grasshopper with four transparent wings. The name RHIZAPHIS was then changed at its birth on 28th August 1868 to PHYLLOXERA which literally means 'leaf blaster'.

The connection was soon made between the flying insect and the galls discovered by Fitch in America. It was also discovered that American vines resisted phylloxera attack, which suggested that the phylloxera bug was indigenous to America and that, in their wild state, American vines had developed an immunity to the pest. It was this observation which saved the European wine industry and led to the total eradication of infected vines. European vines grafted on to American rootstocks are safe from the depradations of phylloxera.

Viticulture

The grapevine is one of the oldest plants cited in ancient historical records and has been used in the making of wine for at least 4,000 years. The Phoenicians first introduced the vine into Europe, through Greece and Italy, where it spread to France, Germany and other parts of the continent east and west.

The Egyptians attributed the invention of winemaking to the king-god Osiris, 'smasher of foreheads, master of gracious men, rich in sweetness, and conqueror through love', who coerced by reason, argument and music. He married his sister, the goddess Isis, and this incestuous union produced Horus and introduced the institution of marriage to mankind. But I digress. The Greeks attribute the invention of wine to Dionysus and the Latins to Saturn. Wine was in common use in earlier periods among the Hebrews. It was forbidden for what must have seemed like ages in Rome following excesses of bacchic licentiousness. At a later period, wine was not allowed to women. Both Greeks and Romans used to scatter it about all over the tables and floors as libations to the gods, and practically swam in it. The custom of drinking the health of good and absent friends may have originated in this way.

Vineyards are mentioned in the Domesday Book as being common in England, and all abbeys and monasteries kept vineyards, tended in the main by monks from elsewhere in Europe. The wines were described as 'tolerable'. The names of several places in Kent are believed to derive from the existence of vineyards in their vicinity. Today the south of England is where most vineyards flourish, though modern winegrowing techniques are enabling vineyards to survive in Scotland.

The growing of vines in England declined during the reign of Henry II, since England at the time was in possession of many of the fine winegrowing districts of France, most notably Bordeaux. Though winemaking declined in England, the growing of vines seems to have always been one of our talents. There exists in Hampton Court an old and famous vine, declared the largest in Europe. It was planted in 1769 and grew to spread 72 feet (21.9 metres) by 20 feet (6 metres) in a trained and supported area. In one season it can produce 2,272 bunches of grapes weighing 18 cwt (914 kg). The main trunk measures 13 inches (33 cm) in girth.

In the mid-nineteenth century, a Duke of Portland tended a winery containing 70 different varieties of vine at Welbeck near Worksop. If there had been a *Guinness Book of Records* then, the Duke would certainly have gained entry with a bunch of Syrian grapes weighing 19½ lbs (8.8 kg).

Few of these grapes, however, possessed much flavour for winemaking and lacked the sweetness, acids, tannins and extracts to ferment successfully and mature with time. It was the general practice to enhance the flavour artificially by adding such things as bitter almonds, oak chips, orris root, wormwood and rosewater. Colour was enhanced by the addition of dyewoods, logwood, berries (particularly elder), burned sugar and iron. The odd human body that may have fallen in to a vat unnoticed, or by design, was thought by many to improve a vintage. Such practices would infringe today's Trade Descriptions Act, though oak and cherrywood barrels serve the same purpose, in effect, by imparting a 'woody' dimension to what are already rich, fruity flavours of grapes.

Oak ageing is considered particularly useful in New World winemaking, where the grapes produced are richer and riper than in Europe and demand the balance provided by wood. Types of oak are important and experiment with different combinations never ceases.

Vines are tended like pedigree racehorses and are often deliberately 'stressed' by various methods of training, pruning and controlled watering, particularly in dry climates where rainfall is minimal. Stressing adds a 'complexity' to the juice of the grape; what is artificially imposed by man in this way is also enhanced or hindered by the vagaries of nature's seasons, sites and, most emphatically, soils.

Hence the importance of the vintage—an annual crop, subject to a wide range of variable factors: weather, geographical position, the soil and its perpetually changing composition in the vineyard, the moment of picking before or after rainfall, the temperature when the fruit is picked, the cellar where the grapes are fermented, the blend of grape varieties and, in the case of grand wines, the skill of the winemaker and cellarmaster—the artist—and his impulsive decisions before, during and after fermentation. Every single nuance of environment and handling, no matter how slight, is registered by the grape like a barometer, from root through fruit, barrel and bottle, to the palate, where even then it is subject to the vagaries and inclinations of the imbiber and his peculiarities and preferences.

PHYLLOXERA
VASTATRIX
alias
Pemphigus
Vitifoliae
alias
RHIZAPHIS etc.,

GOLDEN October in RHEINLAND

GERMANY

Whatever you do, don't talk about the war. Graacher Himmelreich! Oh! Mein Gotten Dammerung! It sounds like I just did—and that's only a Riesling Qualitätswein—a Halbtrocken from the Mosel-Saar-Ruwer. All around the steep slopes plunging into these rivers and into the Rhine itself, vertical vineyards glow like plunder in the sunshine. This is Goldener Oktober country and the hills are alive with the rich juicy harvest of the Riesling grape. It's the same every year and it's getting richer by the minute.

Late Gothic church spires soar into the blue skies like Werner von Braun rockets—but don't speak about the war. Bells ring out and barges chunder downriver laden with the spoils of another midnight raid. The Bernkasteler Doktor will see you now. Scharzhofberger, mein son! I like the feather in your hat. It looks stiffer than I've ever seen it. It must be a good harvest. Haben Sie einen trinken mit mir. Prost!

Grape-laden trollies swarm with weatherbeaten Polish immigrant workers picking out the rotten grapes to make the finest wine. Many of them are teachers, lawyers and doctors who are allowed to come with a letter of invitation for four to six weeks to earn hard currency. In wine families everyone is expected to go out at harvest time and work, but the younger people seem to have better things to do these days.

German rot. The more rotten the grape the

richer and sweeter the wine. Determined-looking harvesters walk horizontally between the rows like dumpy spidermen defying the laws of gravity. Everything and everyone is well built, solid, reliable and dour. Everywhere you look is a background of glowing steep wall-like slopes and crazy jigsaw patterns of crisscross grids and fancy woodwork on half-timbered houses. You feel as though a fairytale is being told on every street corner. Any minute now armies of Hansels and Gretels will run screaming across the square and disappear into the woods beyond, closely pursued by leather-clad stepmothers swishing whips with a satisfying crack as they rush by. Guten Tag, mein little Liebfraumilch. Don't run away or the

BERNKASTEL

OLD
UNSPOILT
MITTEL-MOSEL
TOWN BANKED
ON EACH SIDE BY
STEEP RISING
VINEYARDS OF REISLING
GRAPES

MOSEL

Ralph STEADman

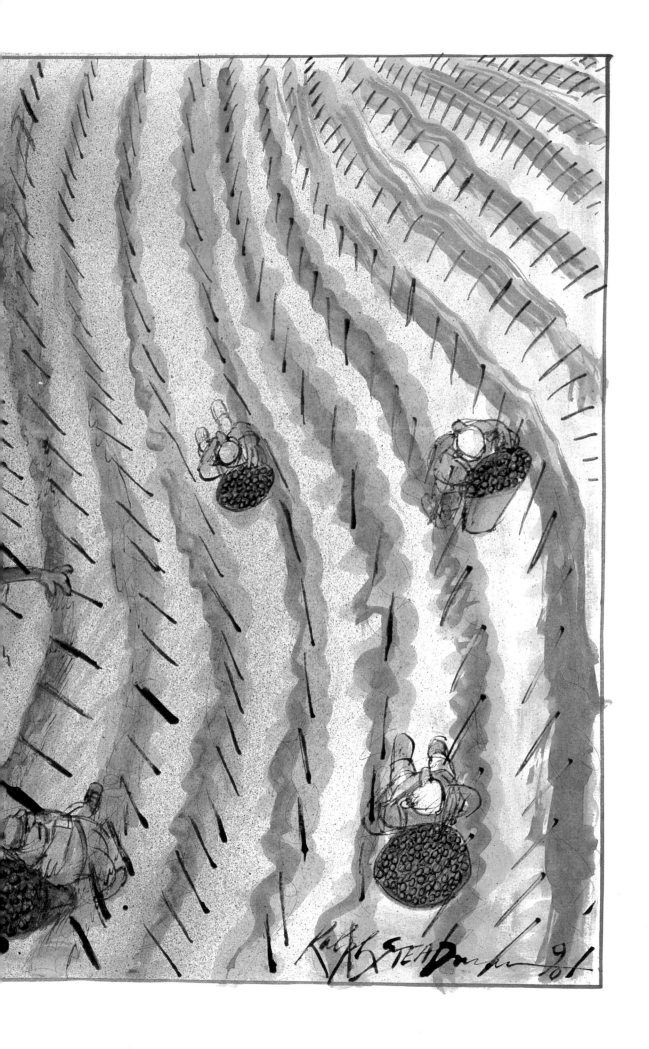

wicked witch will get you. Don't eat her poisoned apples! Do you want to end up in her pot of steaming broth?

The Rhine is distinguished both by the beauty of its scenery and the rich fields and vineyards which clothe its banks. Few rivers in Germany or anywhere else for that matter could attract so many tourists. From Basel to Mainz it flows through a wide valley, bounded on the left by the Vosges, and on the right by the Black Forest and the mountains along the Bergstrasse. From Mainz the mountain ridges approach the river only on its right bank at first, where they form the Rheingau. At Bingen they begin to hem in the left bank also, on past Königswinter they rise majestically in a succession of lofty mountain summits, sheer precipices and wild romantic vistas. Towns and villages nestle beneath it all, and deep evening shadows come suddenly to them like the fall of a giant's cloak.

Towering above on all sides rise rocky steeps and slopes clothed with vines emanating their own golden glow gathered from a day's sunshine. Frequently, castles and fortifications of the robber barons of feudal times gaze disdainfully down from heavenly kingdoms, frowning their impregnability across a landscape locked inside its own breathtaking geography. Such inspiring natural drama attracted many nineteenth-century writers and artists. Victor Hugo paid many visits to the area and particularly to Bacharach, where he recorded much of that gothic mystery in the words and pictures that clothe his work. Turner spent some time there seeking out the subtle rays that hid in darkness. When the evening sun melted all in sight on the other side of the river he found another home for his imagination.

Bacharach, a medieval town built on the strength of the wine trade, glowers moodily in the shadow of the steep vineyards and a windowless gothic church ruin. In the cool, dank cellars of the Weingut Toni Jost, black cellar fungus hangs like vampire bats over massive carved wine casks built like panzer tanks—but we mustn't talk about the war. In the bar restaurant above, a furtive couple sit huddled over a jug of creamy frothing liquid and chunks of onion cake, farting and burping as they drink. This is the first day's partly fermented and very laxative must, Federweise or white feather, much prized by the Germans during the harvest. It gets into the bloodstream faster than a drip feed and scours your bowels like an electric brillo pad. This couple were having their own private festival while we enjoyed our more civi-

lised 1989 Silvaner Halbtrocken which gathers its rich dimension from the sunshine reflected off the river on to the steep slopes, even in shadow. Who can tell what magical mysteries at work there imbue the grapes with such complexities? We can only wonder, and not pretend to know.

'We hate to be chemists,' they say, the Germans. 'We are perhaps biochemists. Chemistry and wine is something awkward and strange. Chemistry is horrible in winemaking. We do not MAKE wine. The yeast makes the wine. We hate to be called winemakers. Bakers make bread. Shoemakers make shoes. Butchers make sausage. But we cultivate vines, we care for the grapes, we pick them at the right time, we press them, we care for the must, we control the fermentation and the yeast that comes with the grapes right into the cask. We then care for racking and filtering the wine away from fermenting products. Then we worry. When to bottle. It is more than chemistry and it is more than just "making". We create.'

'We have to clean our noses, and keep our palates always in good form. With this knowledge we have by smelling and tasting, we know when the time comes for bottling. Yes, there is chemistry. We have to control alcohol, acidity, the sulphur, the density. But this comes afterwards. First of all is our nose and tongue and our mind, which says yes or no. It is to know how to treat your must, to know how to filter, when to filter, and when to bottle. This is the key.'

I was shown grapes on the vine in an organic vineyard in Rheinhessen. If they were my grapes, I would have thought they had gone wrong—but they will use them, that's the filth they need. Rotten and horrible. Like a good cheese board. Winemaking is about putrification, liquid compost bubbling away and oozing gases. The magical transformation of substances from good to bad to rotten to beautiful.

The Germans seem to know better than anyone else how to exploit the grape in all its different conditions. But the emphasis is on white wines. They make perfectly good Pinot Noir reds in the Rheinhessen and other regions, but it does not seem to be important to them. Palates get set in their ways and red wines as a rule are too tannic for the national taste buds. The whole German wine industry is geared with typical German efficiency to the manipulation and control of the Riesling grape, the Silvaner grape to a lesser extent, and Müller-Thurgau, a combination of the above two varieties. Their field of vision is concentrated, but that does not mean narrow. Their

Golden Rheingau   Ralph Steadman

The RHEINGAU at 200 km per hour from the back seat of a Mercedes   Ralph Steadman 90

systematic control produces an extraordinary spectrum of different wine tastes and qualities.

'What you often have with Eiswein, the rare crème de la crème of our wines, is Gorgonzola, blue cheese, or just a very fine liver pâté. Wunderbar! Kaiser Wilhelm for his last wish wanted to have a glass of Eiswein and they gave him Bernkasteler Doktor, the best they had—and he didn't die.'

The Germans prefer to do as much as possible before fermentation rather than treat the finished wine later. They prefer not to disturb it, but one thing they must do is to take the proteins out of the wine, otherwise a haze would remain in the bottle. For this they use fuller's earth or bentonite, which comes from America. It absorbs the protein and precipitates it, and is a completely natural product. It absorbs smells as well. Bentonite must be stored with care. If it is placed near an oil tank or a farmyard the wine will acquire these smells by a mysterious aromatic osmosis.

'Drink the Rheinwein and pickle with the Moselwein.' So the Germans say about their own achievements, but it's all a matter of taste. That is just a little in-house German joke, but the Germans don't joke about their wine, or anything for that matter, so I guess they mean it. Rhine wines generally have more body than Mosels. Mosels are more acidic, lower in alcohol, and sometimes have a natural effervescence or spritz.

Maybe the Germans concentrate on their few varieties to compete with a burgeoning international market. To breed a new variety takes 30 years' work. There have to be many trials. A man can spend his life developing one variety and usually after his death his children find it's the wrong one and have to start again. That would be nearly as good an idea as passing on all your bad debts.

Die Weingut Bruder Dr Becker, organic winegrowers, Lotte and Hans Pfeffer and baby Tillman—from memory, October 1990.

Weingut Tony Jost. Bacharach (Mittel Rhein)

Herr und Frau Jost in die WEIN KELLER
Ralph Steadman

Tafelwein

Tafelwein is the wine that Mercedes advise you to use in an emergency to top up the brake reservoir in the rare event of a disc brake leakage caused by a temperature burst at boiling point because you have just seen the whole of the Rhine valley over a period of six hours at 200 km per hour. Its only other use is to scour reclaimed bottles from a garden shed that have contained some unknown and highly suspect solution left there since before the Second World War.

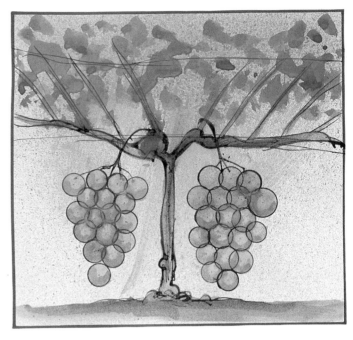

Qualitätswein

Two types. Qualitätswein bestimmter Anbaugebiete or QbA and Qualitätswein mit Prädikat. The first is supposed to be a quality wine from one of eleven specific regions and may be chaptalized (sugar is added to the must to increase the alcohol content). The second should be a quality wine of distinction; it cannot be chaptalized. It is a natural fine wine and will obviously be more expensive—though the degree of difference may be so slight on the palate only the pocket will tell you how to appreciate it.

Kabinett

The purest wine made from normally ripened grapes. Lighter than other wines, it is never chaptalized. It is a testament to the winegrower's care and attention through the growing season and the winemaker's knowledge and skill during fermentation—often one and the same person—Heinz or Kurt or Rudolph or even Herwig but never Kenneth or Brian.

Spätlese

The word means 'late picking'. There is a story that the Abbot from the Schloss Johannisberg always had to give his permission before the monks could pick the grapes. In 1775 he happened to be away at a synod meeting and the harvest was early. The monks sent a messenger to ask the Abbot's permission to pick and by the time the messenger returned the grapes were really getting overripe. The monks harvested with heavy hearts but it turned out to be one of the best vintages ever.

Auslese

Auslese is a method of picking out grapes which have been infected aristocratically with the noble rot, cossetted as they are within the bosom of a whole bunch of grapes which have spent the season striving to be perfect but which are merely ripe. An Auslese grape is the anti-social outsider with the fine pedigree.

Beerenauslese

Beerenauslese is an even more rarified form of Auslese. The grapes (Beeren) are also affected with (or by) noble rot but are more noble yet and sweeter. They produce dessert wines of rare and expensive quality. The finest will always be made from the Riesling grape, but a cheaper yet acceptable variety is sometimes available from the Müller-Thurgau or other grapes.

Trockenbeerenauslese

Trockenbeerenauslese is made from raisined or dried grapes which contain a high concentration of sugar, producing honey-sweet wines of great longevity and breathtaking expense. If you do find some back-of-a-lorry situation staring you in the face, just buy them, lay them down in your cool bank vault and forget about them until your daughter's wedding when you will be grateful for the spare cash you can realise for them.

Er—Liebfraumilch

Over the last two decades Liebfraumilch has earned the distinction of being the wine you ask for when you don't know what to ask for—rather like asking for Kleenex when all you want are paper hankies. Consequently it took all of German ingenuity and efficiency to keep up with demand. Brilliantly the German winemakers rose to the occasion and developed a technique of growing the grapes inside the bottles and through the season allowing them to fill up with rainwater. Snip! and they are ready for corking—and if you believe that, you'll believe anything. You need a sense of humour to devise a scheme like that, and the Germans exercise theirs productively, precisely, and with the utmost efficiency.

Dribbling Noble Rotty Grot
A very rare occurrence, this, but come a heatwave in the middle of December, the odd shrivelled bits of grape left hanging on, after all possible variations of harvests have been plundered and exploited, explode with rich puscillating squelches and oozing promise to create a festival of rich syrupy Grossetrocken or Dribbling Noble Rotty Grot. The last time this happened was 50 years ago, but we mustn't talk about the war.

Spätertrockenbeerentrockenbrunnenspätausenbeeren-auslese
Even later still German winegrowers beat the stuffing out of what is left on the vine until a sickly dried blodge of bruised nothing is left hanging lifeless on a bare thread of limp stalk. Fom this they make wine? It is early days yet but eventually they will get the truth out of this poor grape if it takes them another 50 years. They have ways . . .*

* Footnote
A Winepicking Frenzy for the last vestiges of any-thing vaguely resembling a grape or even a smear of organic sludge that might once have been a grape is sought out by wild-eyed dishevelled casual labourers masquerading as impoverished zealots sifting through mountains of coal-dust for the odd lump. A Black Festival is held after this harvest to consume the juices which have already fermented into a potent wash. The festival takes place on the steep slopes and degenerates into a vine-gnawing orgy when all the general wild pruning is done in the midst of outrageous black humour and celebration, using only the teeth. Old people find it difficult, practically impossible, to hold on to vines on the steeper slopes and so many sacrifices are made, though quite involuntarily, but the soil is enriched and life goes on as it must.

Winemaking in Germany contradicts every-thing I was ever told about the process. That is that you must use no bruised or imperfect fruit. Along the Rhine they disprove that very rule. In Cali-fornia, though, with Chardonnay at least, they take out infected grapes and use only the healthy fruit. That is very American. They are obsessed with hygiene. If they want a botrytis-flavoured wine they'll contaminate the grapes under con-trolled humid conditions to encourage the fungus. They would never dream of letting the stuff run rampant like gossip in a whorehouse.

In the organic vineyards of Rheinhessen they grow clover and lucerne between the vines and tend it like a lawn, letting it rot back into the soil as green fertiliser when they cut. This green carpet also maintains moisture retention, and is an effective preventer of soil erosion. It makes sense

Eiswein

A precious wine of concentrated sweetness—made from grapes taken from the vine when the outside temperature is at least −8°C (17.6°F), for which a winegrower must watch and wait 24 hours a day. The usual time is around 4 a.m. and alertness is a vital ingredient. The grapes must also be ripe enough to be able to make a Beerenauslese wine—that is a German rule for this kind of wine and there can be no cheating.

Auslese Grape 'picker outers'
Separating the noble-rot-infected grapes from the general
bunches of Riesling grapes in the Mosel district of Bernkastel—
the acute mountain vineyard known as the Berkasteler Doktor,
which gives the wines a particular personality due to its extreme
situation and slatey soil.

to me. The rooting systems of such plants are near the surface anyway and don't take goodness from the vine, ultimately going back into the soil as compost.

Ye shall show and ye shall tend
And only they shall harvest when your back be bent.

Most vineyards are less than 34 years old, and some no more than 15 or 16 years. Germans keep a clinical watch on the development of their vines and then very occasionally in the changeover will try a new variety.

Germans thrive on regulation and no other label on the market gives you as much information. Only up to a certain sugar level are they allowed to call a wine dry or medium dry. They are fastidious to a degree. Nothing is sloppy or rule-of-thumb.

But they are not all made of stone. They put their Mosel in green bottles because it is like a young girl, fresh, light and fruity. They put their Rhine wines in brown bottles because it reminds them of a ripe older woman, mature and warm. And that's only what the women think. The men talk of thrusting leather tastes, the edge of a whiplash freshness, and the smooth undulating pulse of a yielding thigh.

The story goes that a Kaiser was in Ingelheim which is opposite Johannisberg, on the other side of the river. He saw the snow melting very early in springtime and he thought this must be a perfect place to grow grapes. So he ordered the first vineyards to be planted. That place is now called Schloss Johannisberg. It is one of the Rheingau's most important vineyards, producing the most expensive wines. How the Kaiser described them can only be guessed at.

Many German wines are chilled before bottling to precipitate the tartrate crystals and prevent them from doing so in the consumer's refrigerator. These harmless crystals are often confused with broken glass or sugar by the newcomer. It is another example of German efficiency in anticipating and eradicating a possible problem.

Germans don't talk very much about complexity but more of different methods of making a white wine from the same grape. The complexity, therefore, is in the variety and not in the wine itself. When I mentioned this to a director at St Ursula, an important wine producer across the Rhine from Schloss Johannisberg at Bingen, he replied that complexity only applies to heavy, tannic wines. Germans speak more of structure, and describe the structure of a wine as a kind of skeleton—the backbone of the wine. I didn't mention the body because he was already getting excited just talking about the bare bones. And the smoothness of the wine was getting to us as we looked over the wide breast of the mighty river. That too was smooth—smoother than a Mercedes travelling along an autobahn at two hundred kilometres an hour.

Frau Jost, Weingut Toni Jost, Hahnenhof

We don't use any poison or insecticide on our vines to kill the bugs. We have special things against these animals. We use special kinds of smells, synthetic sexual smells. The insects are attracted by it and actually come into a trap like we use bottles of jam for wasps.

Nick Schritz, St Ursula

As long as Robert Parker is as powerful as he is and as long as he rates all wines on a scale of 100, as long as everyone wants wine to be in the scale of 100 and as long as a consumer only goes to the shop with the Wine Spectator *under his arm, looking for the wines with the most points, then winemaking won't change because winemaking can't afford to change.*

On the steeper slopes of the Rhine you had better take your lunch with you otherwise you won't get any. Getting back up the hill after coming down during a lunch break, you can forget it.

Heinz Frank, Managing Director, St Ursula

What we know for sure was that the first vines cultivated in Germany were red. The Romans brought them. Then they realised that these red wines didn't become red enough, which is why we plant mainly white.

We are not the enemies of complexity. I think complexity is used more with heavy, more tannic wines. We rather speak of structure than complexity and try to describe the structure of wine like a skeleton.

Big Helga
A nineteenth-century wine press noted for its sensitivity when crushing grapes. The immense size allowed for hair-trigger balance through the pressure range, allowing for that very last drop of sugar-rich juice at the highest pressure without bruising. *This megalith, one of the biggest yet most delicate presses ever made, is now in the Mosel Weinmuseum in Bernkastel and legend has it that this very press gave Hans Christian Andersen the idea for his story, The Princess and the Pea—or was it Grimm who passed the idea on to Hans? Hans*

"BIG HELGA"
19th Century WINE PRESS

MOSEL WEINMUSEUM
BERNKASTEL-KUES.

18 29

Ralph STEADman

was after all Danish, and a teetotaler, otherwise the story may have been originally *The Princess and the Grape*. Or even the *Wicked Witch and the bunch of Pinot Noir* which turned to blood when the fat Duchess dumped herself down on the stained mattress, because the bunch of Pinot Noir grapes was actually a

handsome alcoholic Prince who had been turned into grapes by the wicked witch. Anyway, the Princess was shocked and horrified and asked the Good Fairy to save her Prince, so the Good Fairy turned the squashed mess into a Black Pudding Bockwurst which the Princess loved more than the Prince so everybody lived happily ever after.

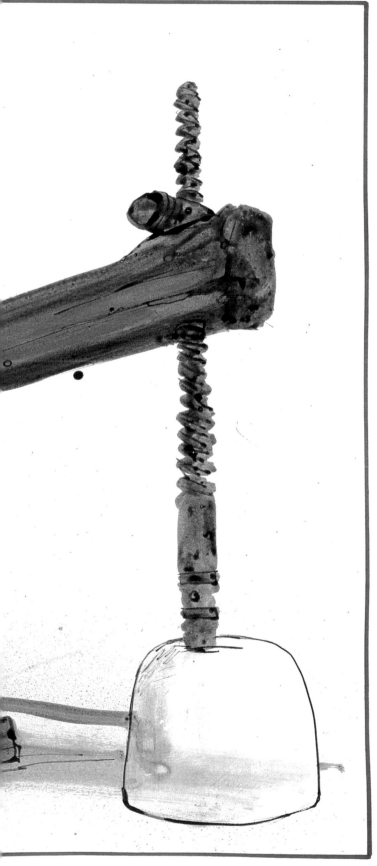

Nick Schritz

The old barrels slowly help to control the oxidization of the wine through the wood and mature it. It is not the intention to give it a wooden taste. If you want a wooden taste then you need new barrels but that does not suit the character of Riesling.

[In the cellars of Weingut Bruder Dr Becker, organic wine growers in the Rheinhessen, the new vintage is bubbling away ferociously.]
Ralph: *Listen to the song of the wine.*

Lotte Pfeffer, Weingut Bruder Dr Becker

It will stay here between eight and 14 days. This beautiful carving on the barrel is the lion from Hessen. Rheinhessen and Ludwigshuhe was flooded every year. The Duke gave money for the people to build the town higher and that is its name—Ludwigshuhe, because the Duke's name was Ludwig and the village is now about ten metres higher.

Elizabeth Stitch, St Ursula

A Trockenbeerenauslese is a sweet wine made with berries that are shrivelled like raisins. If you chill it down to about five degrees and drink it with a Stilton or a really sharp blue cheese it is sheer poetry.

Bury me beneath a vine
And let me pour my soul in thine
(who said that? circa 1992).

The Legend of the At-Least-Seven-Headed Dragon

according to the BOOK of REVELATIONS

And God said: 'Let there be Rhein', and there was silence in the heavens and behold the Rheingau was blessed even unto the Mosel and Saar and Ruwer and all their tributaries from Baden in the south to the land of Ahr in the north. And God made suicidal slopes of great and punishing steepness and these he called vineyards. It was given to men of square determined stature with grim reliability and efficient ways to work and tend these slopes and gather the harvest. God saw das ist was gut and he rested.

And his voice broke out of the firmament again and said: 'These are the words of the óne who holds the seven spirits of God, the seven stars; I know all your ways. I hold at least seven stars in my right hand and walk amongst at least seven lamps of gold that shall be your harvest and everything shall be at least seven for it is more than six. My eyes flame like fire and my feet gleam like burnished brass and to you I give the beauty of this vision but once every year and every seven years you shall know a greater abundance than this.'

And the men of square determined stature were full of joy and greatly puzzled likewise by the

Slopes of great and punishing steepness.

strange proclamation but they held their ground even unto the steepest slopes and did not fall backwards.

And God said: 'Occasionally I will cast you on to a bed of pain not more than once every seven years at least, and you shall know that thine harvest will be blessed. I know all your ways and thou shalt get into line, even unto the steepest slopes which were not given to common mortals to comprehend nor manage by sane means. Or I shall come upon you like a thief in the night and you shall not know the moment of my coming, nor will you know the deep secrets of Satan who comes in the cloth of a vinegar fly. But you shall not be polluted and will walk with me in white.

These are my words, the true words of one who holds the key of Helga the wine maiden, when she opens none may shut, when she shuts none may open save with the screw that offers up the contents of your strength, which is small without my command.'

To the men of the lower gentler slopes God said: 'I know all your ways, you are neither hot nor cold. How I wish you were either hot or cold! But

because you are lukewarm I will spit you out of my mouth, and you will say, ''How rich I am. How well I have done. I have everything I want.'' Though you do not know, it is you who are the

most pitiful wretches, poor, blind and naked. In your richness you must buy from me the gold of the seventh year refined in the fire of mine eyes for your vineyards, and fine white clothes to put on and hide your shame and your nakedness and ointment for your eyes that you may see through the thinness of your wines—which shall not improve with age lest you be patient and wait at the door of heaven for the wisdom to understand the complexity of thine inheritance.'

And those who were wretched in their nakedness stood at the door of heaven and looked in and behold, there in heaven stood a throne and on the throne sat one whose appearance was like the gleam of jasper and cornelian and round the throne was a rainbow, bright as a goblet of golden liquid. In a circle around this throne were twenty-four other thrones, and on them sat twenty-four elders, wearing white and wearing crowns of gold amidst flashes of lightning and dark rumbles of

thunder. Burning before the throne were seven torches, the seven spirits of God and in front of it stretched a sheet of glass, like ice.

Four living creatures lay all around with eyes in front and behind. The first was like a lion, the second an ox, the third had a human face, and the fourth was like an eagle in flight. Each creature had six wings, eyes all over, inside and out. They were given to see every vineyard in every direction from Baden in the south even unto the land of Ahr in the north, and they did did not miss casting their eyes on every leaf. And God said: 'They shall be your guide and your Quality Control.'

The wretchedly naked standing at the door of heaven bought all the gold they could from the fires in God's eyes and covered their nakedness in white robes and went about their business with a greater efficiency and precise deliberation than ever before and God saw das ist was gut and scared them a little with seven bad harvests followed by

one good harvest and the men of the lower slopes developed a square determined stature like the men of the suicidal slopes and alles was gut.

And behold, apart from the seven stars in the right hand of God was also a scroll, but no one was worthy to open it, no one in heaven nor on earth.

'Who is worthy to open the scroll and break the seals?' proclaimed Helga the mighty wine maiden. None was worthy enough—not even the lion, nor the ox, nor the thing with a human face, nor even the eagle who pretended to fly.

Within the circle of the elders and inside the circle of the living creatures, amidst my tears, one stood forward who was none of the above, but a lamb with the marks of slaughter upon its being. Of course and behold, he had seven horns, at least, and seven eyes—the seven spirits of God. The lamb took the scroll from He who sat on the throne. Everyone bowed down, the twenty-four elders and the four creatures. The elders made complicated gestures with harps and golden

bowls of yeast, sugar and tannin and they declaimed in voices of great jubilation that the lamb was indeed the one to purchase from God the instructions of the scroll for the making of the best wines, by merely getting slain.

The lamb broke the first of the seven seals and a white horse came forth carrying a crowned rider with a bow—a conqueror. Then the second seal was broken and came forth a red horse, its rider, with a big sword, empowered to take peace from the earth and make men slaughter each other for gold. Then the third seal was broken and a black horse came forth and its rider bore a pair of scales saying—a whole day's wage for a quart of flour—a whole day's wage for three quarts of barley— but spare the olive and the vine, and the olive and vine were blessed. The fourth seal was broken and, whoops! came forth a sickly pale horse and its rider's name was Death and Hades close behind to kill a quarter of the earth by famine and pestilence—and the sword, if that wasn't enough.

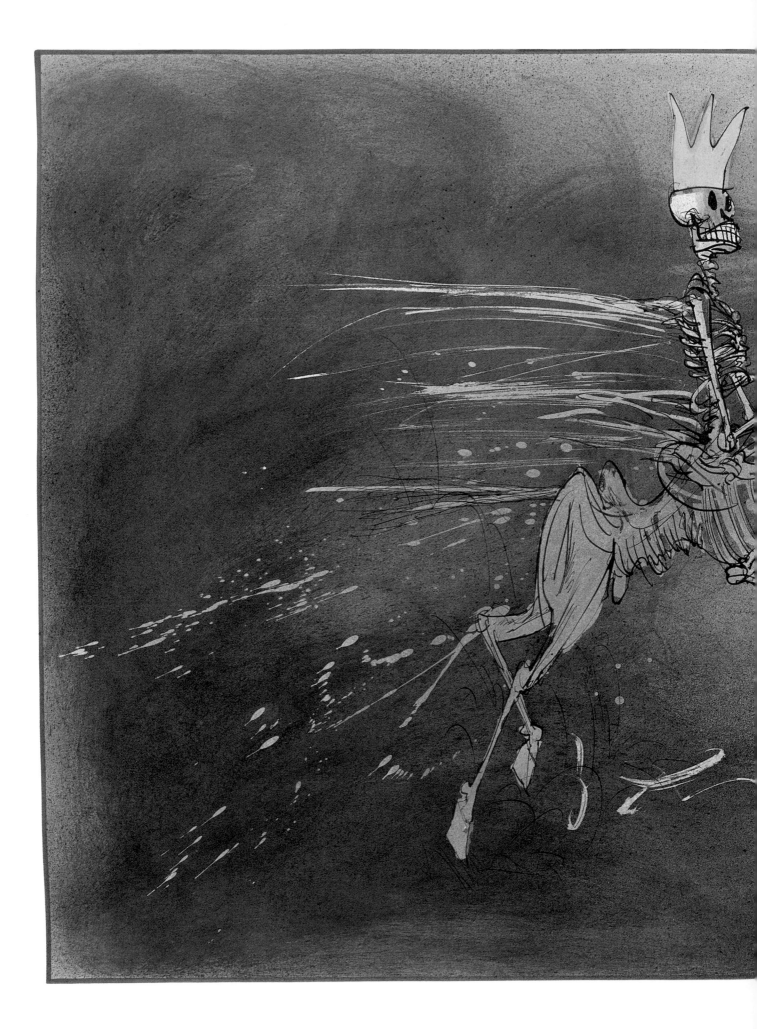

When the fifth seal was broken it was obvious that things didn't look too good and all saw the bodies of the slaughtered beneath an altar, who had given wrong information about winemaking. How long, oh lord, how long, wailed the slaughtered, before we are vindicated and can vent our frustration upon the peoples of the earth with bad harvests? And God counselled patience and dressed them all in white robes.

When the sixth seal was broken all hell broke loose and there was a violent earthquake which caused steeper slopes still. The sun turned black as cellar fungus and the moon as red as Pinot Noir, the stars fell to earth like dead vine leaves, and every mountain and island was moved from its place to where it is now.

All kings and magnates and marshals, the rich and the poor lived in mountain cellars and crags to escape the wrath of the lamb. And four angels kept the four winds at bay from the four corners of the earth. One of the elders turned and said, 'All who have passed through this great ordeal have washed their robes in the blood of the lamb and made them white. Never again will they feel hunger and thirst—the sun will never scorch them—nor their vines.'

Now when the lamb broke the seventh seal, there was complete silence until the angels, now numbering seven, blew their trumpets—except the seventh—and caused all manner of hail and fire and burning and blazing and poisoning of water as though there hadn't been enough trouble already. Even the moon and the sun and stars were struck and dimmed the day and even the night. The eagle flew about the heavens with a woeful squawk warning of more to come. Great clouds of smoke from an abyss poured forth and darkened the earth even more and brought locusts the size of horses with human faces and long hair, teeth of lions and with scorpion stings to torment the poor wretches on the face of the earth who were not yet impressed. There were murderous

angels with squadrons of cavalry with tails like snakes, blowing smoke, fire and even sulphur, which was good for the vines that survived. Behold, there were still some who were hard to impress and did murder, and fornicate and rob even now, and did not repent.

And God said: 'Right!' and sent a mighty angel down from heaven, even worse than the rest, covered in cloud, with a rainbow around his head, a shiny face and legs like pillars of fire. He came bearing another scroll. He planted his right foot on the Rhine and his left foot in the vineyards. He also had a voice like seven thunders which spoke of further violent purpose from the new scroll. But he was restrained from stating it, for the message was becoming clear. God was mad. Someone had to eat the scroll because it tasted like honey in the mouth and like sourness in the stomach and to prove it someone did and proclaimed—'Yes, it's true. This will be the cornerstone of all our wines from henceforth and with square determined stature, grim reliability and efficient methods we shall forge a variety of rich and fulsome difference.' So it was decided upon—after a little more trouble and strife.

At last, the seventh angel blew her trumpet and heaven was laid open to reveal God's act of covenant—and a portent in heaven, a pregnant woman standing on the moon and robed in the sun, pleading to be delivered.

Suddenly, the at-least-seven-headed dragon appeared and hoped to eat the new-born babe and rule all nations with an iron rod, so God took it as an example of the finest harvest that man could strive for, and every seven years God shows it to man.

War was waged on the dragon by the angels of heaven, and Helga was saved from its wrath by eagles's wings. And the dragon spewed a flood of water to sweep her away, but the earth opened up and swallowed the flood, so he went off to wage war on the rest of mankind who eternally fight him off to this day by offering him part of each harvest which has at least seven faces—and all from the same grape. The rest is history.

A Fungal Disquisition

CLADOSPORUM CELLARE is a black fungus which thrives in the humid airless conditions of dark cellars. It is part of an extensive family of cryptogamic plants, generally known to us as mushrooms, toadstools, rusts, smuts, mildew, and bunt. Somewhere between algae and lichens you will find such a fungus.

Practically all fungi are parasitic, drawing their nourishment from the plant or tree on which they grow. *Cladosporum cellare* grows on dark, dank walls and, in such a situation, can barely be called parasitic. Fungi are found all over the world and proliferate in moist temperate climates, living off decaying vegetation and animals. Even man does not escape and is subject to a visitation of fungal growths on cutaneous disorders. Fungus lives on bread, vinegar, paste, yeast, preserves, mustard, corn, potatoes, cheese, berries and damp timber. It also lives on grapes in beneficial and ruinous ways, and worse, in as many as a dozen different species at once.

All fungi are cellular. They form no woody fibre or complex tissue structures like plants, and neither do they contain chlorophyll. Despite displays of extraordinary colour and growth patterns, their composition is a uniform texture of simple cells which give off a reproductive seminal dust. This dust is, in effect, the seeds, but it is actually composed of individual cells. From these arise delicate, minute cobweb-like growths called the mycelium. This mycelium penetrates and destroys the object on which it feeds. Although soft and spongy, fungal growths are able to lift heavy stones under which they may form. Unlike plants they absorb oxygen and exhale carbon dioxide like human beings; like humans, they can be either nutritious or poisonous.

I wasn't going to bother you with this information but fungus is fascinating stuff. The black mildew, *Cladosporum cellare* or Capnodium, is classified under HYPHOMYCETES. This order includes the multitude of minute moulds which appear on any surface prone to dampness. In the case of wine cellars it acts as a kind of interior decoration, nurtured with pride by a cellar master like a display of battle scars. The bigger the scars, the older the cellars and the richer the tradition. These are the attributes that every winemaker yearns to possess as his background and heritage along with dust and cobwebs. Probably the best bit of his CV is his CC. Somewhere in there is a twinkling clue as to why an elegant bottle of fourth growth Château Prieuré-Lichine from Cantenac-Margaux goes so well with a wooden board laden with mouldy old cheeses and a chunk of French bread.

St URSULA Weinkellerei WINE PRISON for RARE VINTAGES / Bingen (RHEINHESSEN) VILLA SACHSEN RalphSTEAD

Note the CLADOSPORUM CELLARE — The black cellar fungus thriving under intensely humid conditions. No decent self-respecting cellar should be without it

PORTfolio

**Factory House Dinner, OPORTO,
Portugal. 25th September 1989**
The evening was to be a spectacular event. A kind
of send-off occasion before embarking on a week-
long tour of the Douro valley vineyards. Many
leading port makers, merchants, mayors, council-
lors, glowing noses, ill-fitting suits and flunkies
crowded into a bust-lined lobby leading to the
main banqueting hall. Aperitifs were being served
as we waited for dinner (in honour of the Whit-
bread company) to begin.

Our team had been invited by Sandeman and our host was Manuel Ferreira, the Export Director. We entered the banqueting hall to be seated around a long table with elegant semi-circular ends bedecked with cut-glass tableware and silver candelabras, in a chandeliered room dripping with damask curtains, wall tapestries and oil paintings of porty people from long ago. The cold white aperitif port liberally ladled out by the flunkies in the lobby now made conversation cheap and easy. I was seated next to Manuel. On my left I believe there was a woman but I can't be sure. I was deep in conversation with my host about port and comparisons with other kinds of drink.

'At some point something dies,' I was saying, referring to the moment when brandy is poured into the fermenting must to halt fermentation, which makes it an entirely different kind of drink from ordinary wine. Manuel nodded.

'It must be something to do with the level of contemplation, understanding, subtlety, tradition and everything that goes with port,' I continued. 'The chemical magic inside a grape makes wine a living substance which continues to ferment, whereas with port that moment when fermentation stops is rather like an electric shock which denatures the characteristic qualities of wine. I believe that some wine enthusiasts don't like port for that reason.'

'But some people have lived with port and cared about it,' replied Manuel. 'They have been brought up in the atmosphere of a port-making family. There is a tradition. They are above the public mentality in such matters. They inherit a legacy. In some ways they must maintain a strange, mystical quality and a certain distance from an outsider. Perhaps they can't really explain the attraction of the process or even the process itself, so the knowledge remains intuitive.'

The conversation was better than the food. Factory House food is rather stodgy and very English. Colonial food would perhaps be an apt description. The wines, however, were Portuguese, a Chardonnay, Quinta de Valprado 1987 and a warm aromatic red, Celeiros 1978. I particularly like Portuguese wine and this was excellent.

The trick of the evening came after the fruit pudding with port sauce. We were all asked quite suddenly to stand and move through a large pair

of doors at the end of the room into an identical room, except that the only picture on the wall was a picture of the Queen over the fireplace. There was also an identical table with identical candelabras and decanters of port ready for dispensing. Watching our hosts for helpful signs regarding decorum we resumed our places, in exactly the same positions as next door, but now with cut-glass port goblets in front of us instead of fruit puddings. The neatness of the move preserved the ambience that had been generated during the meal. It was obviously a well-practised habit.

It dawned on me that we were about to toast the Queen and after-dinner speeches would be forthcoming. By this time it hardly-mattered and I was ready to speak my mind into a haze of cigar smoke and the glug-glug of the passing port.

There came a moment when I felt the urge to stand up and speak, so I did. Unloading my mind haphazardly upon a startled throng, I swayed back and forth and gesticulated like an excited kangaroo:

'As an unbeliever—wines and ports—ladies and gentlemen. Port—I think port is an, an entirely different kind of drink. Biggest dinner party trick I ever saw just happened—one minute we're sitting with our pudding plates—I'm not a pudding man myself—trying to catch the wine waiter's attention—suddenly everyone is getting up and bingo!—we're in the gun room right next door. I expected the women to go somewhere else, but here we all are—how nice! Exactly the same but in an adjacent room, just like a frame on a film. All of us back where we are—but with a glass of port in front of us—must have done it before—like a first-division football team, and the room still throbbing with nostalgia and well-oiled tradition—all of us still jabbering away being nice to each other—instead of being tempted with seconds, nice as it is was, roast beef and spinach, all very English, *very* English. And there she is—the Queen.

Something that struck me today is that certain things which have been done over the centuries must have been done for a reason. The reason is either to perpetuate something that may be good for some people, and not too good for others—er—or perhaps still good for a lot of other people if that lot of other people could have had the same privilege that we have had tonight. All this grandeur—wonderful stuff—but I must point out—outside—all that shabbiness—what a shame—a walk around the streets this afternoon left me shocked. A beautiful town, but falling apart like an old temple to the gods—what happens to all the duty from the sale of port? Maybe the government could spend a few bob on the streets, but—er—sorry, just an observation—not a criticism. The idle chatter of a stranger—um—I—er, I'm still wondering at this point about—what is port? And when does it stop being wine and become port? There is a moment when that happens and when it happens it's like lightning. The introduction of the brandy is an adulteration—a stab in the back of a warm and living nectar—an act of necessity perhaps—at a time when England was losing its control of French vineyards in the seventeenth

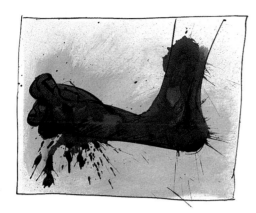

NOVICO NORMALIS. The average foot of the casual labourer. Very little of the foot is used only . . .

The HEAVY DUTY or PROFUNDO is a foot to be reckoned with and can often mush two kilos of grapes in one stamp. Very popular for the non-vintage years when the harvest is plentiful but not special.

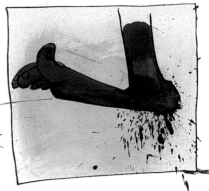

O CALCANHAR—the heel is a brutal tool used only on the hardest of skins—creates a bitter taste—the crush is too severe for a fine vintage crop.

The FINO PÉ or THIN FOOT can only be effective on small harvests since most of the grapes are simply missed by so fine an area of pressure. Owners of feet like this have been known to resort to the buttock press or BUMLADO in desperation, but many have drowned attempting it.

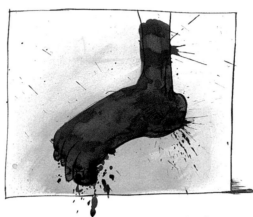

THE ARCHED TRIOMPHO adopted for the most delicate crushing where 1 in 12 grapes are fully crushed and juice and tannin are extracted in varying degrees from the other eleven. This creates complexity in the wine of dazzling confusion.

THE COUP DE GRAPE. The master of the trade has such a foot, and sometimes even two. A gnarled ballet masterpiece, its owner can command the price of a square meal anywhere up the Douro. These feet can dance into the very heart of the grape.

century. Portugal's new commercial alliance with England in 1703 was the open door England needed—did you know that? Never miss a trick, the English. Portugal is a long way from home, yet we could not abandon our addictions. Fear of future deprivation justified the adulteration—and guaranteed safe exportation—and forged this English corporation! So this illustrious English Factory House was born, a fitting centre for the new masters of the market the English were to become, and practically the only imbibers of this rich resilient aberration called port. But the tentacles of England were spreading around the globe and with them went port, strangely now an English drink, the drink upon which the sun never set. To help ward off degeneration while building up colonialization, we toasted our deliberation—by arresting prolonged fermentation. Port and Empire! To Port and Empire!!'

I toasted the Factory like the buggering fool I can be on such occasions.

'But I digress. The wine, for it used to be wine, depended nevertheless on all the usual unavoidable variables to create the raw material, the humble grape. Weather, humidity, mist coming in from the sea, oozing up the Douro valley, winding like a whisper of loose gossip, curling through the patient vineyards, as Dylan Thomas might have put it, rather better than me. Never mind the poetry. All are important factors—while the grape is still a grape. So, the grape is important. Couldn't use a gooseberry, could you?' Anna catches my eye and is looking at me nervously. But I stumble on: 'So even after the addition of

Trail Blazer Port Bottles.

Novelty Style.

Full Bodied + Robust

Uncertain Vintage.

RICH RUBY PO

BRAWNY PORT

Light Aperitif.

Perfumed Souvenir Silver Jubilee.

Portuguese Man's War.

brandy, the moment when port exists and wine stops—wine still persists through the drink until it finally becomes what I'm not sure it is any more—if you get my drift—the wine must surely project its qualities, even though it is not a spirit, not a wine, but a port.

And that's the problem with port. It makes you go on a bit. And port does go on a bit, itself. Some ports go on for a hundred years and way beyond,

undrinkably. So having said what I've said for what must have seemed like a hundred years of dispensation of my erroneous conversation, I thank you for our invitation. Thank you and sit down please.'

My speech was spectacular, not for what I said, but for what happened next. I sat down and my chair collapsed into bits.

Luckily it was one of those old ones, about 200

years old, and obviously full of woodworm. Fourteen flunkies rushed forward to help me to my feet and I stood for a moment, startled, looking about me at everyone. No one knew whether to laugh or look concerned. Another seat was brought which caught me with perfect timing.

After one or two historical speeches about the origins of the Factory House and the medieval Latin word *factoria*, which has something to do with business transactions, the port was passed again and the Queen, who was by this time was reminding me more and more of Mary Poppins, was toasted.

I kept coming back to that nagging point about what port is. Manuel Ferreira said it is neither a wine nor a spirit. It is an essence. He made it

CHAIN HUMPING A BARREL. A chain is attached to the bung on the inside of an empty barrel and a small amount of water is added. The lads then get bumping backwards and forwards over a hump of clay-like sand in a concrete pit. It is the oldest but most effective barrel-cleaning method known.

sound more like perfume. However, it is the continuation of a process, even a life. But which life is it continuing? The life of the spirit or the life of a wine? I became fixated by the stage at which a wine dies and a spirit takes over when the brandy is added. Having stopped the fermentation you do not stop the maturing process, the spiritual content of the wine, and I think 'spiritual' is the right word, because the essence grows towards the spirit, but yet something dies with the brandy. Something dies between the two states. I feel a strange ambivalence towards the drink. I cannot feel the same emotional response to it as I can towards wine.

Some say it is like strong wine. But I can't drink it like wine. I can't even drink it like spirit. The world outside Portugal has not been educated in the ways of port—except through English gentlemen's clubs, and other exclusive institutions. It appears that it must be drunk with a set of ingrained procedures. Passing the port at a certain time to toast the Queen is *de rigueur*. Toasting

other noteworthy individuals or established institutions seems to occur to most port inebriates when in their cups. Nobody, it seems, toasts the inhabitants of cardboard cities, or police violence, or refugees, or even the under-privileged generally on any side of the fence, which of course is not the Queen's fault in the universal scheme of things. But it does lend a certain amount of unease to the ceremony of passing the port in this day and age, if you are the slightest bit aware of such problems.

And yet we learn that white port can be drunk chilled as an aperitif, lightly, and with a certain *joie de vivre*. Even as a refreshing summer drink—which seems to be something of a contradiction, and that's what worries people. They feel, perhaps, as though the decorum is an essential part of the enjoyment of port, and therefore to drink it without decorum may cause embarrassment. This adds to the underlying resistance from the general public; they are more likely to put it in the trifle than bother with the intricate rigmarole of its drinking ritual. Paradoxically, I hate the rigmarole, and I hate trifle. It takes me back to the days when I used to have to eat acres of lettuce 'to do me good' with a half-inch blob of salad cream; and jelly—which I was only allowed to enjoy with a couple of slices of pre-buttered bread. Nothing was to be enjoyed for itself. That would smack of self-indulgence.

The whole image of the drink needs reassessing and subjecting to a public relations campaign, if the public are ever to overcome the long-held notion that it is always the port that gives them a headache the morning after the night before. From what I have learned in Oporto it appears that port has so many different styles, it can be adapted to suit many occasions otherwise reserved for the lighter drinks like champagne or sparkling wine. The special combination of magic and ritual could perhaps be emphasised. It's fun, in the right frame of mind. Why not? There is really no point in denuding life of all its frippery. Passing the port in a clockwise direction is classic stuff, a piece of theatre. But at present it's only associated with gentlemen's clubs. Port is not a woman's drink either, yet, unless it is drunk with lemon, Coca-Cola, or Benylin—yes, Benylin. And if you think *that* one is weird, how about trying it with tomato juice?

Michael Symington of Graham's told me that if you wanted to open an office on the Oporto side of the river Douro, back in about 1750, when the Factory House, centre of business transactions in the port industry, was being set up, you would

Port-blending frenzy

have had to pay a levy to the Bishop of Oporto for the privilege. In order to avoid that levy all the major port houses simply set up shop on the other side of the river, at Vila Nova de Gaia, which is why that is where all the port lodges are today.

In 1910 the government suggested that instead of paying the Bishop, such a levy should be paid to the government, and it insisted that those companies in Vila Nova de Gaia should do the same. Today all port companies pay the government a levy per litre of production. From that levy the government are supposed to give at least half back to the city of Oporto for renovation and administration. But there is little evidence to show for the renovation side of the deal.

There is no duty paid to the government directly on alcohol sales in Portugal. If you have 20 vines

'MOMMAS': Port Storage Vats. Quinta do BOMFIM, Douro Valley. Ralph Steadman

'MOMMAS': *Port Storage Vats. Quinta do* BOMFIM, *Douro Valley. I was shown the strange otherwordly tanks which store bulk ports before they are taken by road tanker down to Vila Nova de Gaia. They are made by inflating large balloons and covering them in fibreglass which in turn is covered in cement. The balloon is then extracted and the top is capped. A door for cleaning is set in the side and they are painted white to reflect the heat of the sun and prevent the contents overheating.*

And then, on the very same morning, I was shown the stock of pigs they breed specially to feed the workers who harvest the grapes.

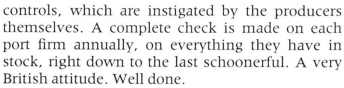

behind your house in Portugal, you can make the wine and set up a stall by the side of the road to sell it. The government imposes duties on bulk shipment of port for export which is high, and on bottle shipment for export which is lower. Again, a proportion of the money is supposed to be put back into publicity for the Port Wine Institute, which controls and supervises the entire output of the region.

The Institute itself, however, is very strict in its

controls, which are instigated by the producers themselves. A complete check is made on each port firm annually, on everything they have in stock, right down to the last schoonerful. A very British attitude. Well done.

A few of the vineyards up in the Douro still have, in place of modern presses, old-style granite *lagares*: flat shallow baths set into the steep slopes and covered over by crudely built stables. The *lagares* can accommodate about eight brawny

Portugese footstompers arm in arm, wearing tartan shirts and denim blue shorts. Together with a spot of squeezebox music, the grapes are pressed underfoot and the crushing work is transformed into a joyful festival. Using gravity, the juice is run off these treading tanks down runnels like drainage gutters into large casks. Farmers are given authorisation cards by the Casa do Douro which allows each farmer to make a limited amount of port annually, depending on the quality category

in which his vineyard has been placed. Money is advanced on a kind of banker's credit loan system from year to year, depending on the quantity and quality of the harvest, which over the years accumulates or depreciates. The farmers are at the mercy of the vintage and dependent on the large merchant houses which sell the port. This may not be such a raw deal for the farmer, but it does keep him in his place.

These communities of farmers, however, are

fairly self-sufficient, and work, eat and sleep on the job, watched over by the land-owning families with a proprietorial air of patronising British benevolence.

In picturesque dwellings set into the hillside hollows, buxom, sturdy women cook at stoves and open fires, surrounded by the dead vine wood piled up in the kitchen, used for stoking the fires. Casual labourers who transport the grape-filled

hoppers to and fro, up and down the vineyard slopes in the heat, sleep in rude huts among piles of potatoes, a staple diet. The hoppers are supported on their foreheads by straps which are attached to the base of the hopper. An expert can carry a loaded hopper without holding it steady with his hands and a punishing rhythm of going back and forth is maintained effortlessly throughout the day.

The flag is never lowered; for there is always someone, somewhere in the world drinking Port

Douro Valley, Sept. 89

...of every day and night — Elizabeth Symington

At the end of the harvest, the whole community collapses into a bacchanalian celebration—music, laughter, dancing in the vineyards and general groping horseplay erupts like an uncoiling spring, spilling humanity everywhere. There is a simple beauty in it all and an earthiness which reflects the very soul and character of the harvest. That is something the pervasive British influence has not yet managed to conquer. To their credit, the British quite enjoy its attractions vicariously, and are proud to welcome visitors to share in the merrymaking. Though some of the workers are students doing holiday jobs and enjoying themselves, it is difficult not to be reminded of that old Victorian song 'It was Christmas Day in the Workhouse'.

You don't go to Vila Nova de Gaia to see a lot of cellars, because the vintage port is under London, not Oporto.

Late Bottled Vintage arose as an alternative to Vintage port. At one time, there was nothing between Vintage port and Ruby port. It was a schizophrenic market. Vintage port is for the very rich and port and lemon is for the pubs—a polarity of the whole social spectrum. Now a middle section of society can drink LBV as an acceptable alternative to Vintage. Whereas Vintage port is bottled between two and three years after the harvest, LBV is bottled between four and six years after the harvest, the extra time in wood softening and taming its character.

Vintage ports are 'declared' two or three times every ten years—only when the wine is fantastic. In the years when Vintage port is not declared, the shippers take the best of their 'quinta' (farm) wines and declare those as 'single quinta Vintage ports'. These mature more quickly and are ready for drinking when they are about ten years old. They cost the consumer about half the price of a Vintage port, and are only put on to the market when they are ready for drinking. By contrast Vintage port is put on to the market when it is young, and it is the responsibility of its purchaser to mature it for the 20 or 30 years it needs before it is ready to drink.

The Dry White 'Apéritif' Port before Lunch

The Port and Lemon, Luv

The Listing to Port

The Port with Everything

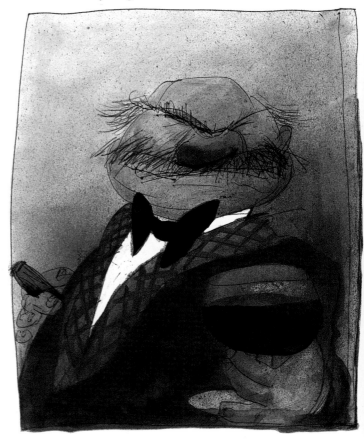

Tawny Port at Xmas.

Founder's Reserve at the Club

The original port was made from juice that was so sweet that sometimes it self-arrested its own fermentation high up the alcohol scale without the addition of brandy.

Brandy was not added as part of the wine-making process at first but merely to give a higher strength to the wine. Originally, basic port, which had to endure a long journey of many weeks back to England, was treated with brandy in stages to avoid it turning to vinegar should it be left hanging around in leaking casks, either during a voyage or on the docks. Higher strength meant a hardier wine.

The drink we recognise today as port goes back only 130–140 years. What William Pitt used to drink three bottles of in one session was simply a strong, dark table wine.

Because it is not possible to excavate cellars into the granite rock on which Oporto is built, port is stored in lodges: large stone and wood warehouses. A fire started in one of them, so I was told, and the whole lot disappeared in 20 minutes.

Despite the pervading English influence that is found in parts of Oporto and the Douro, on occasions the order of things can be dislocated by an unconscious display of idiosyncratic existence.

The image that will stay with me forever is the weird juxtaposition I saw on a high shelf behind a dusty bar in Pinhão, far up the Douro valley, towards the end of a very hot afternoon. It was a stuffed red fox grinning vacantly across the room with its back right leg half cocked over one of two large bottles of Bosford's Dry Gin. It appeared to be backing on to the nearest one with quiet deliberation.

I couldn't keep my eyes off it. I guess I was wondering what the hell it was going to do next. I often ask for a Bosford's in an English pub, but the response I get is a stare far glassier than the one in the eye of the Pinhão fox. I have to make do with a Gordons.

RARE DRINKS Nº. I

British Made

24789

1947 51

Bos ford's
RICH TAWNY
BRIT

Ralph STEADman

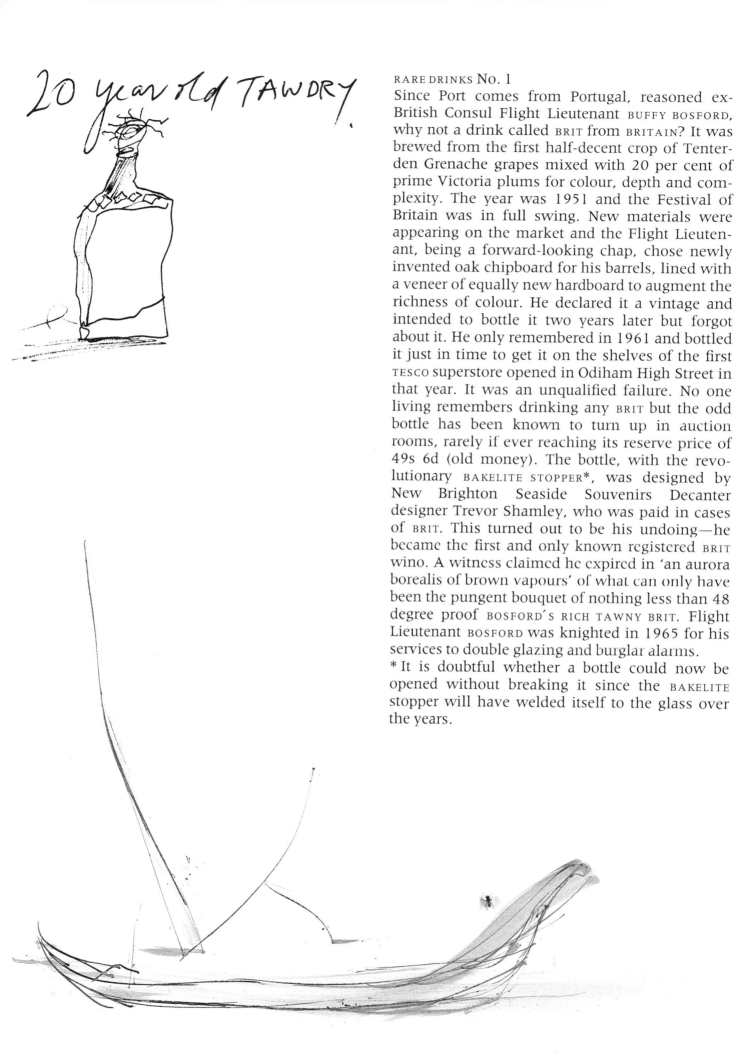

20 year old TAWDRY.

RARE DRINKS No. 1

Since Port comes from Portugal, reasoned ex-British Consul Flight Lieutenant BUFFY BOSFORD, why not a drink called BRIT from BRITAIN? It was brewed from the first half-decent crop of Tenterden Grenache grapes mixed with 20 per cent of prime Victoria plums for colour, depth and complexity. The year was 1951 and the Festival of Britain was in full swing. New materials were appearing on the market and the Flight Lieutenant, being a forward-looking chap, chose newly invented oak chipboard for his barrels, lined with a veneer of equally new hardboard to augment the richness of colour. He declared it a vintage and intended to bottle it two years later but forgot about it. He only remembered in 1961 and bottled it just in time to get it on the shelves of the first TESCO superstore opened in Odiham High Street in that year. It was an unqualified failure. No one living remembers drinking any BRIT but the odd bottle has been known to turn up in auction rooms, rarely if ever reaching its reserve price of 49s 6d (old money). The bottle, with the revolutionary BAKELITE STOPPER*, was designed by New Brighton Seaside Souvenirs Decanter designer Trevor Shamley, who was paid in cases of BRIT. This turned out to be his undoing—he became the first and only known registered BRIT wino. A witness claimed he expired in 'an aurora borealis of brown vapours' of what can only have been the pungent bouquet of nothing less than 48 degree proof BOSFORD'S RICH TAWNY BRIT. Flight Lieutenant BOSFORD was knighted in 1965 for his services to double glazing and burglar alarms.

* It is doubtful whether a bottle could now be opened without breaking it since the BAKELITE stopper will have welded itself to the glass over the years.

Lanzarote

Lanzarote is the most north-easterly of the Canary Islands, and lies about 90 miles (145 km) from the African coast. It is only 36 miles (58 km) long with a mean breadth of 15 miles (24 km). It has a rugged coastline of high basalt cliffs rising in some places to 1500 feet (457 metres). There are mountains inland rising to 2,000 feet (610 metres) and they are all volcanic. The soil is naturally fertile and can in rainy years produce great luxuriant crops and foliage followed by years of drought and desolation.

However, Lanzarote does possess something unique—the most unusual vineyards in the world. They flourish in the strangest conditions on flat volcanic plains in a region known as La Geria. The Lanzarotters grow their vines in concave bowls below ground level on the plain's surface for two or three reasons. The plains are subject to high winds created by extremes of temperature. The vines could not survive the battering that they would inevitably receive, nor would the grapes withstand the intense heat of a midday sun. The concave bowls provide a modicum of shade at different times of the day and re-radiated warmth at night when temperatures can plummet to near freezing. Apart from that I know nothing, except that the wine produced from the grapes is called La GRIPPA. It has a volcanic edge, bores holes in the back of eyeballs and drives men into the arms of strange women who wait like traffic wardens at a rock-concert parking frenzy. It is not mentioned in any *World Atlas of Wine* as far as I know. Nevertheless, La Grippa has a certain ring to it and as tastes broaden will one day find its niche in the growing international markets of wine.

Lanzarote Vineyards, in for the wine 'LA GRIPPA'.

of La Geria, Canary Islands.

Ralph STEADman 9.

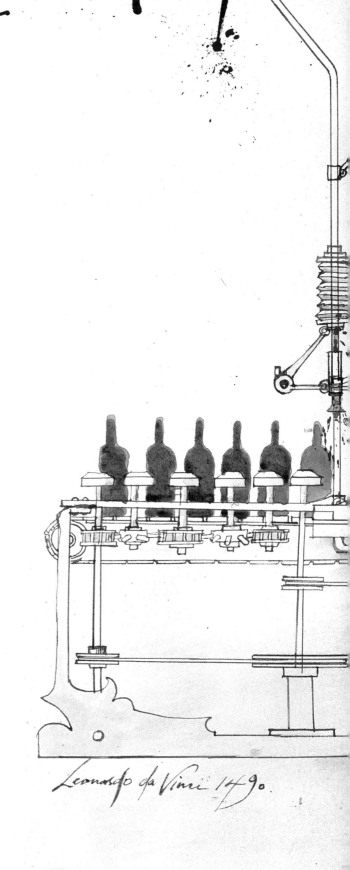

Leonardo da Vinci: Thoughts on Wine from one so divine

I take a vessel filled with wine and I draw off the half and fill it up again with water: in consequence the vessel will contain half wine and half water.

Then I draw off half again and then fill up with water, wherefore there remains, etc.

Since every continuous quantity is divisible to infinity, if a quantity of wine be placed in a vessel through which water is continually passing it will never come about that the water which is in the vessel will be without wine.

If a cask is filled four braccia high with wine and throws the wine a distance of four braccia, when the wine has become so lowered that it has

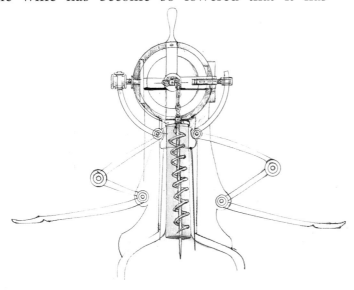

How you may withdraw the longest of corks from the most illustrious and delicate bottled wines in your darkest and coolest cellars with such ease that her divine ladyship may do it for your discerning lordship.

Leonardo da Vinci 1490.

How thine illustrious wines
may be placed in bottles for
thine own cellars, and thine own
pleasure_____. (Memo to Il MORO.
Ludovico Sforza.)

dropped to a height of two braccia in the cask, will it also throw the wine through the same pipe? i.e., whether the fall, and the range that the pipe can throw, diminish in equal proportion or no.

If from the cask when full, two jugs are filled through the pipe in an hour, then, when the cask is half full it ought for this reason to fill only one jug in an hour, if pouring from the pipe. (One braccio = two feet) (NOTE: This principle is the basis of all modern plumbing).

TO ADD WATER TO WHITE WINE AND SO CAUSE IT TO BECOME RED

Crush an oak apple to a fine powder and stand it for eight days in white wine, and in the same way dissolve vitriol in water, and let the water and the wine settle well and become clear each of itself, and strain them well; and when you dilute the white wine with the water it will turn red. (English winemakers trying to make red wine in uncooperative climate take note.)

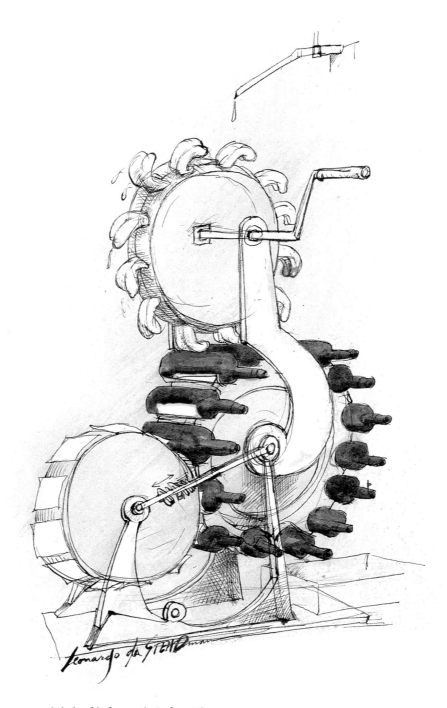

How you may moisten many labels of information about the contents of the bottles to which they will adhere. Leonardo da Steadman

Wine, the divine liquor of the grape, finding itself in a golden richly chased cup upon Mahomet's table, after being transported with pride at such an honour, was assailed by a contrary feeling, and said to itself: 'What am I doing? What is it that I am rejoicing at? Cannot I see that I am near to my death, in that I am about to leave my golden dwelling in this cup and enter into the foul and fetid caverns of the human body, to be there transformed from a sweet fragrant nectar to a foul and disgusting fluid? And such an evil not sufficing, I must needs lie for a long time in foul receptacles with other noisome and putrid matter evacuated from the human intestines.'

It cried to heaven demanding vengance for such injury and that an end might be put to such an insult, so that, since that part of the country produced the most beautiful and finest grapes in the whole world, these at least should not be turned into wine. Then Jove caused the wine which Mahomet drank to rise in spirit up to the brain, and to infect this to such a degree as to make him mad; and he committed so many follies that when he came to his senses he made a decree that no Asiatic should drink wine; and thus the vine and its fruits were left at liberty.

As soon as the wine has entered into the stomach it commences to swell up and boil over; and then the spirit of that man commences to abandon his body, and rising as though towards the sky it reaches the brain, which causes it to become divided from the body; and so it begins to infect him and to cause him to rave like a madman; and so he perpetrates irreparable crimes, killing his own friends. (I once had a wine like that.)

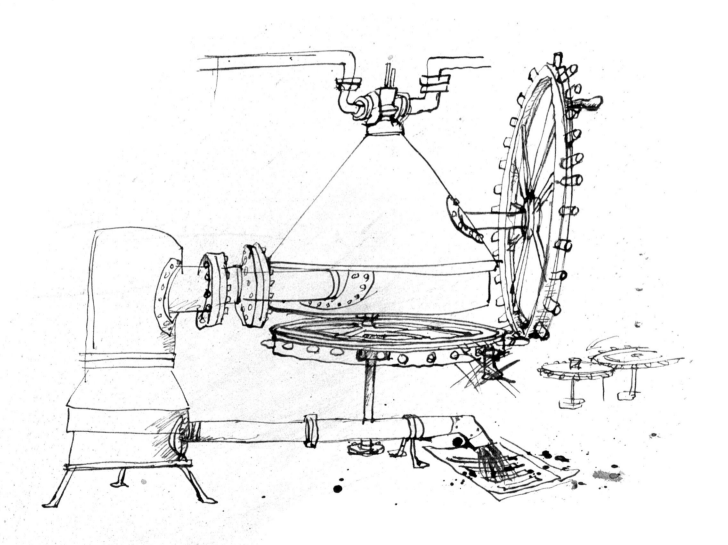

How you may centrifugally disperse sediments and impurities from a new wine.

Roman Vineyards, CAREMA. N.W. Italy 18th Feb 1990.

GIACOMO BOLOGNA, Barbera producer of the flat plains west of Milan and creator of the fine Bricco dell'Uccellone, and friend of itinerant fiddlers whose escapades of fantasy and surprise can be imagined and relived every time a cork is drawn from one of his bottles. What?

GIORGIO ALIATA, the booming high priest of NERVI'S GATTINARA wines of Piemonte (mountain foot) in north west Italy. A masseur of the noble NEBBIOLO grape he teases out its very soul and treats every wine like a prodigal son returned.

The spider had placed itself among the grapes to catch the flies that fed on them. The time of the vintage came and the spider was trodden underfoot together with the grapes.

The vine that has grown old upon the old tree falls together with the destruction of this tree. It was by reason of its bad company that it failed together with it.

OF LEATHER BOTTLES
The goats carried wine to the cities and great rejoicing came to those who met the goats at the gate and escorted them to the city square.

Be temperate with wine, take a little frequently, but not at other than the proper meal-times, nor on an empty stomach; neither protract nor delay the visit to the privy.

Wine is good but water is preferable at table.

If into a vessel that is filled with wine as much water is made to enter as equals the amount of the wine and water which runs out of it, the said vessel can never be altogether deprived of wine. This follows from the fact that the wine being a continuous quantity is divisible to infinity, and therefore if in a certain space of time a particular quantity has poured away, in another equal space of time half the quantity will have poured away; and what is left is constantly being replenished with water; and thus always during each successive space of time the half of what remains will be poured out. Consequently, as it is capable of being divided to infinity, the continuous quantity of the aforesaid wine will be divided during an infinite number of spaces of time; and because the infinite has no end in time there will be no end to the number of occasions on which the wine is divided. (Leonardo had another shot at explaining this theory when he was sober. See simpler version on pages 122–124.)

LUIGI FERRANDO, *wine maestro from the Roman vineyards on the rocky slopes of* CAREMA, *nudging the French Alps in north west Italy. He makes wine with the earthy enthusiasm of an amateur and the masterly passion of an orchestral conductor enshrined in the modesty of age-old customs.*

Count PIERALVISE SEREGO ALIGHIERI, *descendant of* DANTE *himself, whose quiet charm belies a* vignaiolo *with a dreamer's ambitions. His estate also houses the first Agricultural School of Oenology in Valpolicella founded by his family 50 years ago, and is the flagship of the MASI wine company which creates wines from* CORVINA VERONESE, RONDINELLA *and* MOLINARA *grapes that only dreams are made of.*

Salai, my wayward apprentice, did entice beggars right off the street. I covered my embarrassment with tricks to entertain, for to be fair they had been promised food and drink in exchange for posing in my *bottega*. I was bound to tell them the coarsest anecdotes to please their fractured minds. And this I did besides: if I poured wine into a bowl of heated oil the alcohol flared up and burned before their eyes. (This anecdote suggests that wine in the fifteenth century was stronger than wine is today, in general. A flashpoint of at least 45 per cent alcohol is required to ignite a Christmas pudding with a lighted match, even surrounded by inebriates who have been drinking for three days straight in close proximity. The 'wine' Leonardo mentions was probably distilled Chianti from the grapes of vines grown on the lands owned by the Borgias, whose wars did away with thousands of fertile men and women. They were ploughed into the Tuscan soil as rich food for thought and agriculture.)

The Valtellina

The Valtellina, as has been said by many, is a valley surrounded by lofty, daunting and terrible mountains; it produces a great quantity of strong wine but has so great a stock of cattle withal that the peasants reckon that it produces more milk than wine.

It is this valley through which the Adda passes which first flows through Germany for more than forty miles.

In this river is found the grayling that feeds on silver of which much is to be found in its sand. Everyone in this district sells bread and wine, and a jug is never more than a soldo, veal is a soldo the pound, and salt ten denari and butter the same and eggs a soldo for a quantity. (Leonardo maintained a household of two apprentices, a blacksmith, a cook and several horses on a meagre 37 ducats a month in Milan at a time when Michelangelo was earning 1000 ducats a month in Florence and Rome.)

VITTORIO BORATTO—*Mr Caluso Passito, so named for his exquisite and honeyed sweet wine made from semi-dried* ERBALUCE *grapes grown around* CALUSO *and* IVREA, *north east of* TURIN. *He also has the distinction of having the most probing nose in the business.*

SYLVANO PIACENTINI, *managing director of Instituto Enologico Italiano, whose taste it seems is to unify the multivinous activities of the Italian winegrowers and create a force to be reckoned with. He is a kind of broker and he can break a bottle of Giuseppe Quintarelli's Amarone della Valpolicella 1983 over my head anytime.*

EZIO RIVELLA, *King of the* CASTELLO BANFI *wine company of* MONTALCINO, *Tuscany, whose benign manner and warm hospitality mask a serious business brain and the organisational powers of an ant colony. His* BANFI *wines are as strong and exquisite as the* CASTELLO POGGIO ALLE MURA, *a castle with a dungeon cellar of fine wines, the centre of his kingdom.*

GEROLAMO BAZZANAROLA, *whose aesthetic ideas of winemaking have now largely died out thanks to the new enlightenment and quality control of DOCG. But in his heyday people listened to him and followed his example — which was the next best thing to spraying your vines with* PHYLLOXERA. *His ideas, in fact, led to the now famous 'Bonfire of the Vineries' when all the vineyards of Western Europe went up in smoke to purge them of his pestilence.*

Castello Poggio alle Mura.
(Villa BANFI) SIENA.

ANGELO GAJA, *the Lorenzo de Medici of Italian wines. He runs his superb estate in Barbaresco, north west Italy, like a king runs his Rolls Royce. A perfectionist from the heart, his wines are now acknowledged as being among the world's greatest tipples. When he speaks the world of wine listens.*

The SAN GIMIGNANO *of the Italian wine world whose many wine makers pride themselves on the length of their corks.*

GIUSEPPE QUINTARELLI, *the poet of Valpolicella, who has the coldest cellar I have tasted in and one of the warmest intuitions it is possible to be blessed with. He can discover in a grape dimensions that can make Verona's Roman arena look like a multi-storey car park.*

SAN GIMIGNANO *is a hilltop town in Tuscany where once seventy towers were built, each much higher or lower than its neighbour—depending on the greater or lesser importance or power of the family building it.*

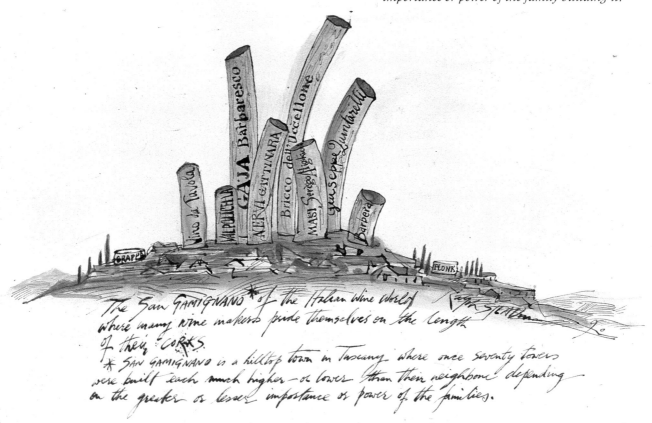

Angelo Gaja

Sometimes visitors to Italy think that Italians have too little interest in their traditional varieties. It is not because we are forgetting them. Maybe the problem is that in foreign markets we meet difficulties in proposing local wines. It seems easier to propose a Cabernet Sauvignon. We have more than 240 different varieties. It can be a problem.

With my winemaker, Rivella, we started together to review tradition. We analysed each step and we kept what we believed in. In the traditional process there are some things that we can believe absolutely that are perfect today and some others that belong to myth because technology has changed. We added some things we believed were important to create a style for a world class wine, not a wine to be liked necessarily.

We can look to the future but at the same time we have to remember the land and the climate which are permanent factors. The man sometimes cannot change totally but can modify a little and give a new interpretation.

In Switzerland there is a very important chef near Lausanne. I have known him for ten years. I was there with a food writer. The chef created some fantastic dish with a lot of fantasy, beautiful things and colour, very provocative. I went there again with my family four or five years ago and then last June and I saw his style had changed towards more simplicity. Not being with the food writer, he was not stimulated to be provocative. The food was extraordinary, so fine and so simple. To arrive at this simplicity is not by chance. You have to have all that experience, all that creativity to be capable of repeating time and time again.

Winter Scene. NEBBIOLO Grapevines – NERVI Estate – GATTINARA facing N.E towards SWITZERLAND
Ralph STEADman 90

The Wine in Vinter

Villa Banfi 1989, at Villa Roma Imperiale

This was a pleasure anticipated, a celebration, at our hotel after a prizegiving ceremony in Forte dei Marmi. The wine was offered to us to taste and sprung like mustangs from the glass. Even the waiter disappeared in an opium cloud of sheer ecstasy and I nosed the glass for what must have seemed an eternity to everyone else hanging on the tip of my nose like expectant fledglings. The stainless-steel palace of computerised production which is Villa Banfi in Brunello de Montelcino, a place we have visited, came into my mind in the form of a fairytale castle and I was transformed. Unfortunately, *so was the waiter; he had disappeared, and eventually returned with the nectar. Horror! The fool had decanted it into one of those flat glass monstrosities that give the impression that the dregs of something long gone are upon you. The delicate structure and balance of the Villa Banfi wine had been disturbed and scrambled as surely as if he had shaken a bag of eggs. I was mortified but polite. The wine was poured and nevertheless enjoyed, even though the effect was like Tosca performed on ice. To confound the frustration we ordered another bottle of the same but this time insisted on it staying in its natural home, taking it at our leisure.*

Italian wine is complex. More complex even than the gesticulations Italians use to express themselves. Not only in its structure but in its variety of grapes, growing areas, methods of fermentation and passionate opinions. All of this, positively undulating in a multitude of microclimates in mini-kingdoms that even Cesare Borgia failed to unite.

To a born-again novice like me, Italian wine is very difficult to come to terms with, and even more difficult to remember. In fact, I'll come clean—all I remember for sure is that Valpolicella is made principally in the north east around Verona. A very sweet wine known as Recioto is made from grapes dried on bamboo racks, and a drier, more bitter version called Amarone, with a hint of spritz, is made using the same technique. Barbera and Barbaresco come from the north west region of Piemonte around Asti (sparkling wine, too) and Alba (Barbera, and the most hideous block of concrete it was ever my misfortune to spend a night in). Chianti, meanwhile, is produced in the mid-western region of Italy known famously as Tuscany, heart of Renaissance Europe, including Siena, Florence and Pisa, and now probably the heart of the Renaissance revival in wines perpetrated by the small grape grower/winemaker, inspired by the maxim that to make a good wine you need a good client. What goes on in the other, southern, two thirds of Italy? Don't tell me, let me guess. Mainly white wines like Frascati, a favourite of mine, of gentle strength; Trebbiano, a sharper white; and Sangiovese, an extremely light red which I have always tended to avoid.

The far south of Italy is still a region of mystery to me and its wines can only be a voyage of discovery at some future date. Marsala, a kind of sickly sweet sherry, is the only Sicilian wine that I have heard of, but logic alone would suggest that there are surprising palate-ticklers yet to find in such a sun-blessed region.

Italy has responded to new world markets opening up, and the developing palates of growing armies of wine enthusiasts demanding quality and individuality. This Italy once had generally and has maintained through its individual masters like Quintarelli from Verona, Gaja from Barbaresco, and the late, great Giacomo Bologna from Asti.

Thanks to them, and others like them, the Italians have clawed back their self-respect. The shock of scandal that billowed like a rotting spectre in the early eighties, the damning clamour

of additives added to 'support a wine's structure' and poison the new wine-swilling public became the spur for the Italians to reassess their two-litre plonk image.

It awakened the refinement in their dormant souls which Dante damned in *Il Purgatorio* and Leonardo da Vinci reinvented in thoughtful reflection, invention and pictures by declaring that without the soul we are all mere passages for food—and wine, I guess.

Winemakers have rediscovered the complexity of a single grape variety (and there are hundreds to choose from). They have rediscovered themselves and the knowledge that within such raw material, which grows in overwhelming abundance, they can be individuals again and create a wine that is a reflection of themselves. Individuality is the key note under the controlling umbrella of the DOC (Denominazione di Origine Controllata), established 29 years ago.

To achieve recognition, the grape grower must be a decent winemaker who consistently achieves a standard of excellence. After that, a true artist can excel and create a classic wine from his own combination of variables—weather, soil, growing methods, geographical position and native chemistry based in principle, it seems, on pure intuition. The intention of DOC is not, as I originally assumed, the imposition of a controlling body which serves only to make all Italian wine the same. On the contrary, it maintains a common bond of quality. This serves as a foundation upon which an individual can build his idea of what a fine wine should be.

I suspect that the Italian temperament, that explosive mixture of passion, nonchalance and impulsive classic style, really needs a marshalling agent to concentrate its wilder genius towards a common goal.

The wines I tasted during my stay in Italy were without exception delicious—but I fear that they may be the ones that I could never afford to drink back home. Some Valpolicellas I have bought recently left me clutching at my throat and reaching for a Setler. 'Aaaaaargghhh!!!' I gargle, as I stand bolt upright in the middle of a formal sit-down dinner, eyes bulging and now clutching my stomach.

'Who put the POLICE in ValPOLICEIla?' I croak, looking desperately from guest to guest. They stare back at me in total horror. They know exactly what I am going to do next. I've done it before. I stagger backwards and grab desperately at the table cloth as I fall. Instinctively, to a man, they all snatch their respective corners and hold on like grim death to prevent a major cleaning bill. I am held stiff and diagonal, like a ramp-launch missile at the ready, until the acid spasm passes.

'That was close,' I whimper. 'Panic over. Relax everybody. Put on another Pavarotti.' Gentle hands support me into my seat and the searing pain subsides. Every time I reach for my glass nine pairs of hands snatch at the table cloth, so I retract mine and play sheepishly with my food. Friends now know that only the best Valpolicella Classico Superiore from villages such as Gargagnago, Marano, Purano and San Floriano will suffice. Anything less is simply inviting disaster in a monstrous trough of embarrassment. It works every time.

Count Pieralvise Serego Alighieri [*looking at an old picture in his kitchen*]

That's the Bishop of Verona with my grandfather. The people in this area think that if something needs to be done, it is always better to have the Bishop on your side.

Guide at Masi vineyards

The Veneto is a smooth region. In the countryside you will not see high mountains, but you see a lot of hillsides. People are smooth, not so sharp, kind people but also with a nice temper, hard workers, but they like very much the life, the family and the traditions. The wines are the mirror of the country and the people.

Renato Trestini

To sell a good wine you need a good client.

Before DOC regulations I remember being thrown out of shops in England because I used to present wines that cost £1 a bottle and they would laugh. But what kept me going was that whenever I did tastings people would say, 'I didn't know that Italian wine tasted like this.'

Steve Daniel, Senior Winebuyer, Oddbins

The Italians love to break rules. I think they will continue to make their own wines. Wine is always about the guy who produces it.

Luigi Ferrando, Winegrower, Carema

Villa Banfi makes good wine because it has the best wine maker in Italy and there is no problem of money for producing good wines, always good wine, good wine every year. It is like a company that produces computers.

Castello Banfi. Country.

Angelo Gaja, Winemaker, Piedmont

All fruits are different. You can't find a grape that gives you everything.

Renato Trestini, Wine Agent, London and Italy

To start a vineyard these days you have to be wealthy. If you want to make a small fortune in wine you have to start with a big fortune in something else. In Tuscany a lot of industrialists from the north want to have wine so they buy a farm by a small village and they get the machinery and an oenologist and then they put their name on the finished product.

At the Castello Serego Alighieri the beams are so old they are only held together by the woodworm linking hands. It is the oldest winegrowing estate in the world, and the present day owner's ancestors go back to Dante. Dante's son bought it in 1343 for 450 lire.

With cork you can never be one hundred percent sure that it isn't damaged by weevils. That is why I have been debating for years that the best way to have a wine bottle is with a ring-pull designed by Leonardo da Vinci. All this nonsense about wine having to breathe. Why should it breathe? You put it in a cellar where you have dead rats, leaking gas pipes. If the wine breathes it can't possibly make the wine better. The secret is to have perfect closure. You would really be surprised after five or ten years how exciting that wine could be.

Now take a cork with all its muck after ten or 15 years. Draw it, put it in a glass, pour the wine on top of it and then ask someone to drink it.

1 'Earing' the wine. The sign of a true connoisseur of Italian wines. Before even 'nosing' the wine, a taster will 'ear' it for any sounds of cries for help, a grape in distress, perhaps, beaten and brutalised at the time of picking and during the first few days of fermentation. A good taster will go no further if he 'ears' the slightest hint of these malpractices.

2 Secondly, and still before a drop has been tasted, an expert will 'eye' the wine for signs of bruising in the colour. This will show up on the side of the glass as smears—not to be mistaken for 'legs' or 'tears' which are telltale signs of structure denoting a fine wine. Smears are smears and give you the uneasy feeling that the glass is unwashed.

3 After 'eyeing' the wine, it must be 'spun' to release its imprisoned delights. 'Spinning' must be executed carefully if the wine is not to end up in your neighbour's lap or on some wine critic's notepad and that is tantamount to earning a total ban from all wine tastings. The elbow technique is a skill requiring much control before attempting it.

4 Finally, the 'sip and suck' technique. After another cursory 'nosing' and an 'eye' against the light, the wine is sipped and then air is drawn in through puckered lips, vapourising the locked-in aromas which then invade the palate. The sounds produced during this ritual vary between a tummy rumble and a duck releasing wind under water.

The 'lunge and spit' following tasting depends to a certain extent on the experience and the excellence of the wine, though often a polite silence reigns supreme, even if you feel as though you are savouring a shot of ammonia. It is the sign of a real novice to make too many oohs! and aahs! or to say 'Cor, that's a good 'un!'. Simply observe the reverence and imagine that you are taking Holy Communion. To a connoisseur it is a religion and a fine cellar is his church.

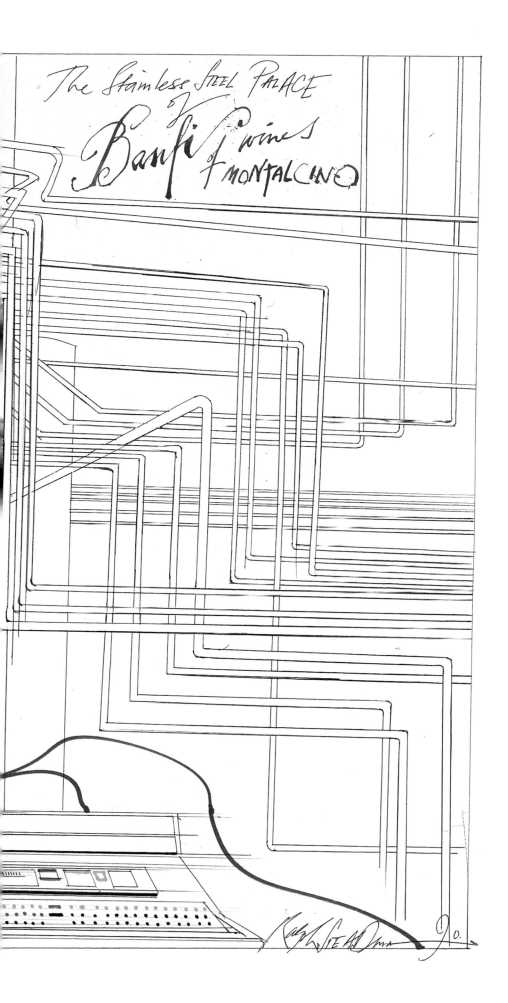

The Stainless Steel Palace
of
Banfi of wines
of Montalcino

CLOSE UP OF WRITING ON DUSTY BOTTLE, VINTAGE 1967 from the cellars of Castello di BANFi— Author's idea for new line in labels.

Brunello di Montalcino 1967

Serègo ALIGHIERI
WORKMAN'S LAST SUPP
Ralph STEA

The MENACE OF ITALIAN BREAD STICK FANATICS—Verona, 24th February 1990

Angelo Gaja

I know a man who smokes 80 Gitanes a day and when he is tasting he smokes four or five and he is still capable of splitting the smell into 40 or 50 different categories. Fantastic!

Wine goes with food. Wine writers are used to judging wines without food. That is suffering, you know.

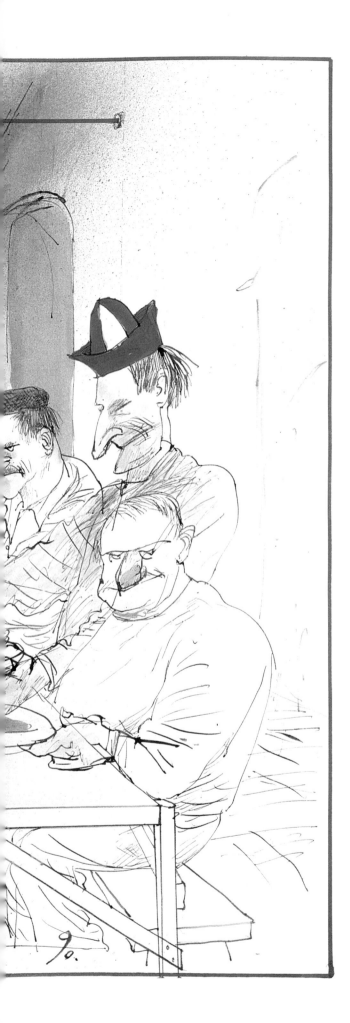

The New Italian elongated, triangular, round, semi-circular square meal, in rich sauce. Alba, 17th February 1990

AUSTRALIA

A vintage visit to the wine baths of Southern Australia

Homage to AUSTRALIAN WINE inspired by
ABORIGINAL ART — the only true
culture to emerge from the AUSTRALIAN
continent in the last 40,000 years.

Ralph STEADman 9

Sometimes I don't think the people at Oddbins take wine seriously. It's just a game to them. They smile all the time and laugh like drunken jesters, tossing names like Latour and Pétrus around as frivolously as they would plastic beach balls on bank holidays. Here they are, guiding even the greatest of wine buyers like myself through the steaming swamp of mysterious regions and appellations as though they were treating me to a free ride on a big dipper. 'Wine is fun!' they shriek, and blow another party whistle in my face.

But to some poor souls it's damn near a religion. Some true lovers of good wine, with nostrils like Formula One exhaust pipes and palates as sensitive as any erogenous zone, build shrines in their cellars to their greatest acquisitions. They don't just 'put' wine there, they 'lay it down' like caring lovers. They lower their voices and whisper years and château names like priests taking Holy Communion—which maybe in some ways what they are.

There is something pretty impressive about 'nosing' the first drop from a freshly opened wine of your very own choice poured reverentially in front of your spellbound table audience—and then sending it back because you can smell musty cork. That's power; and since that's the way real connoisseurs would have it, then there ain't a thing anyone can do but bring another bottle.

When Oddbins asked me to go and see how things work in Australia, I thought I would be in for a rougher, readier ride, where they would perhaps knock the top off the rarest wine on the edge of the table and swig it like thirsty drunks. On the contrary, they are as bad as the French about wine. Wine and love are synonymous and

Rod, Penfolds Nuriootpa

The boys are smelling the fermentation all day long. They are always a little bit pissed.

[Sound of a kookaburra]
That's Johnnie Wirn. His father used to do it as well. He's never been out of the state. Three years ago he went in for a raffle to win some beer. In fact, he won an overseas trip to Europe for 15 days. He was so worried about the travelling he never went.

Ayers Rock Vintage 3,000,000 BC (Ulurouge)

Ayers Rock Vintage 1989

they would like all whingeing poms to know it. If you don't, then they'd just as soon run you out of town tied to a 'roo bar and that's no place to savour a decent drink.

A flight to Australia is very long. Long enough to transform any views one might have had about anything into memories.

When you arrive even your clothes feel out of date, your mouth is a fur-lined garbage container and your body clock is now a time bomb.

By the time you have stumbled through the next 24 hours, your liquidised brain has probably registered the Sydney Opera House, a prehistoric mar-supial lion at the Australian Museum, a kangaroo directing traffic and the quintessence of Australian culture, the 'brown eye', when about twenty apparently sane grown men in shorts and white socks turn their backs on you and, at a given signal, drop their shorts, crouch quicker than you can say 'flash photo', get decent again and carry on talking about their British origins as though nothing had happened.

At this point, consult a doctor and get something to straighten you out, then forget you ever came from England. I had to do exactly that.

We saw a lot of wine country but even this was only a fraction of the massive region known as the Barossa Valley, where dedicated vine growers and

A CORROBORREE by a BILLABONG near the GHOST GUMS

wine makers have mastered their scientific art. The region boasts an army of proud and legendary names which slip off the tongue far better after a few glasses of the very liquid these names represent. Names like John Riddoch, the father of the Coonawarra wine district, who started his career as a fruit grower after acquiring land with money he had made supplying gold-crazed miners with provisions, during the Victoria Gold Rush of 1851. He established the Coonawarra Fruit Colony in 1890.

In his first season in 1891, he planted 95,000 vines in four varieties: Shiraz, Cabernet Sauvignon, Malbec and Pinot Noir, most of which thrived in an area 15 kilometers long by one kilometer wide (nine miles by half a mile) which he subdivided and sublet to different vine growers. This area has the best soils in the region. While the vineyards have grown, the town of Coonawarra remains practically non-existent. There are about as many people living there as you would get on a small bunch of grapes—64, so I am told.

We have been on this flight so long it will probably be 1992 when we arrive in Sydney. When we collect our baggage my flared trousers and wing lapels will be out of fashion and Australia will be Islamic. As it turned out shorts were chic in the best restaurants, corks are passé and the only minaret I saw was in fact a kind of Post Office Tower in Sydney.

DIDGERIDOO— beyond the BLACK STUMP. Ralph STEADman March 1989

Charles
Nettoon.

Nanabanji:
A first
taste of 1951
Grange Hermitage
in the Barossa
Valley, August 1953.

Max Schubert, Wine Supremo, Magill Estate, Grange Hermitage

I was always interested in wine because I loved the smell of it. You know, during the vintage, the smell of the spent skins—I used to savour that.

A lot of early wines were subject to bacterial infection because they couldn't harness the pH. I was the first one to use pH theory down here. Without the pH factor it was very hard to make wine that was proof against diseases. Wine must be quickly balanced for acidity, sulphur, and alcohol. Until you have the proper levels of all these and maintain them above the level at which bacteria grow, you will always have problems.

It was really unheard of in those days to set out to make a wine that would last a minimum of 20 years. So I guess those early bottles of Grange Hermitage are a historical wine. I think that's why it's so expensive and there's very little left.

I can show you a wine list that was given to me the other day at the Intercontinental Hotel in Sydney. They had all the old Granges, and the 1952 is listed at 6,000 Australian dollars. If you've got the money you can drink it there, if you want to.

BIG DOLLY FRINTON *pursued her husband right up to* NORTH QUEENSLAND *and got him making wine out of dusty* MULGA, GIDGEE *and* BRIGALOW SCRUB. *The taste was too radical even for the Australian palate, more used to the broader dimensions offered by* MASTICATED TREE BARK.

MABLE MCCUBBERY: *her husband made his name as the* TOWANG FLOGGER, *handing out corporal punishment across the backs of chain gangs at the* TOWANG *stockade, south of* GOULBURN. *He did the same to his vines and produced a rare vintage. Unfortunately he went soft and lost his touch.* MABLE *never had it.*

Little FANNY BUCHANAN, *'the girl with the cattleprod eyes', who helped her husband to concoct* BOTRYTIS RED ROT *to sell at the Immigrant Reception Depot at Murrumburrah. Upwardly mobile new Australians spurned it as a drink they would rather forget. Little Fanny's*

husband, STUMPY, *hung himself from a dead gum, and* FANNY *lived on to emulate his example as the worst winemaker south of* DUBBO CREEK. *She made a fortune out of* DEAD MAN'S GULCH, *a paint stripper of a brew made from* BOILED PLATYPUS SKINS *and* IRON FILINGS.

BAROSSA PEARL *ran a Catholic soup kitchen for down-and-out* GOLD PROSPECTORS *while her husband, Archbishop* CONNEMARA, *a* BENEDICTINE, *roamed the outback on horseback preaching the evils of abstinence and administering communion wine as an answer to everything from* DINGO BITE *to* DAMNATION.

'LONG FLAT RED', *as she was known, dyed all her dresses in her husband's vintage of '94. He,* 'CUBBY' GALWAY, *sunk his gold into a 50-mile stretch of the* HUNTER *Valley which ultimately became a road. Nothing grew after the first year of '94.* LONG FLAT *buried him in one of her dresses.*

Kangarouge at PLAY.

Samuel Wynn is another great name, the founder of Wynns Coonawarra Estate. I was lucky enough to taste Coonawarra Estate Claret, vintage 1954, and I made some pretentious notes at the time. I had a gastro-enteritic stomach, so I knew this was going to be some test. Its first breath in 35 years hit me fair and square up flared nostrils with the rampant valour of the Light Brigade six hundred sufficient to inspire a poem of some quality even out of the most meagre Tennyson. The taste of wood was thickset and four by two. As it continued on its journey, as much through the mind as the body, the wood became a roof joist able to support a rugby scrum in the room above while the mind underwent a complete reassessment of the laws of relativity. My host, the vintner Peter Douglas, reckoned it had just peaked and from here on in would begin a downward path, leaving an increasingly sharp, acidic aftertaste. If it had been in his cellar, it would have been out of it now and drunk.

'DIGEREE' TENTERDEN thought he had it made with TENTERDEN'S FORTIFIED BOGGO but, like so many others before him and since, he misjudged the new Australian appetite for wine as something akin to SNAKE BITE. He cut off the top of his hat and went mad in the sun.

'WOGGA' STAINES, who planted too many Semillon grapes and had no means of cooling his wines. 'WARM WOGGA WHITE' became a byword for urine and Wogga died a disappointed connoisseur.

BRINDELL PACKSTAFF, an ex-convict, gained his freedom welshing on his mates. He cheated a tribe of Aboriginals out of 2,000 square miles of bush country to grow Shiraz. He became the vinegar king of Adelaide, but died lonely.

BRICE GUMSTUCK grabbed the headlines in the YANCO GLEN EXAMINER with his revolutionary winemaking process. He found that half a pint of CASSOWARY SPIT added to each thousand gallons of GUMSTUCK FLAT RED made wine brewed in cattle troughs taste OAK MATURED and NUTTY. When the YANCO locals sprouted blue feathers and headlumps it was all traced back to GUMSTUCK'S process. He became YANCO's first mayor and lived to be 110.

Another great name, perhaps the greatest, is Dr Christopher Rawson Penfold, a contemporary and friend of Louis Pasteur, who was a great believer in the therapeutic value of wine. Pasteur gave Dr Penfold some vines whose roots had been dipped in wax to preserve them, and he took these, along with his wife Mary, when he emigrated to Australia in 1844. He built a small house called The Grange on a plot of land near Adelaide known as the Magill Estate, and set up shop as a doctor and part-time grape grower. He wouldn't have been the only accidental doctor of mercy or wheat-farm pioneer to try his hand at growing a few grapes, at first just for the fruit, but then realising that with a little more knowledge and control, a far more marketable commodity was theirs to exploit. A fruit of perfect composite parts, sugar, natural yeast and tannin, which, with the help of brandy, created fortified wines—ports and sherries to satisfy a pioneer's palate or resuscitate a pallid straggler who would stumble, sick to the heart, into the waiting room of Dr Penfold's surgery. There he or she would be dosed immediately with a substantial quantity of fortified wine before even seeing the doctor.

By the time they did, things felt 100 per cent better, or at least 18.5 per cent, depending on the strength of the pre-treatment potion. It was not a trick so much as a belief, the belief of Dr Penfold that such wines relaxed and reassured the patient and, furthermore, cured the vexing complaint of anaemia brought on by gut-twisting ailments

GRANDMA SKEHAN *joined her husband,* BANDY, *after a lifetime of Irish waiting, when he finally gave up* GOLD *prospecting and planted vines on a patch of scrub he was given following the* FREE SELECTION ACT *which effectively wrested land from the powerful squatter* LAND KINGS. BANDY'S VINES *turned out to be* POISONBUSH *and he was prosecuted on a charge of mass manslaughter.*

WINDY WENDY McCLAVITEE, *so named as the widow of* WHISPERING McCLAVITEE *whose sparkling white wine was so gassy it blew his customers into the outback on their way through* PENOLA *where they ran a* POSTHOUSE *vineyard.* WHISPERING McCLAVITEE *exploded during a special turn-of-the-century tasting of* NANGWARRY.

associated with change of climate, dehydration, bad water, poor diet, cockroach fever, bad legs, homesickness and scurvy. These stalwart folk must have had the constitutions of desert snakes, or had an intuitive knowledge of foul and pestilential antidotes, for they not only survived but thrived in a hostile land whose only hospitable landmass covers no more than one per cent of the whole continent.

Needless to say Dr Penfold and his wife Mary became well respected in the district on account of their warmth and unique bedside manner.

Dr Penfold continued to develop his winemaking techniques, while Mary had the flair and the driving force to look after the business end.

From a rude hut built in the middle of a plot of strange red soil, one of Southern Australia's major industries grew, and Penfolds has become probably the most distinctive winemaking force in the Barossa Valley. Penfolds Grange Hermitage is acknowledged to be Australia's greatest wine, and it is largely the result of the determination and vision of one man, wine maestro Max Schubert.

His experimental work started in 1951 after a visit to France and other winemaking countries. The Australian palate was not yet awakened to the taste of good quality table wines, and one critic mistook the first 1953 vintage for 'a very dry port—and one to be avoided'. Made almost entirely from Shiraz grapes from the Magill Estate

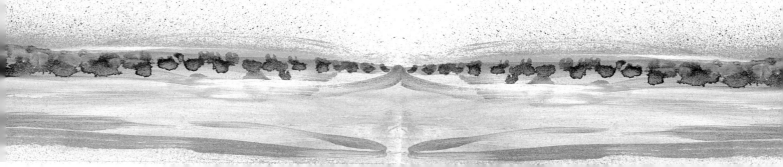

and Morphett Vale, with 10 per cent of Cabernet Sauvignon as a balancing factor, its ferocious depth was disliked and in 1957 Max was asked to cease production. But like all good hell-bent men of purpose he secretly kept a brew going in refurbished old oak barrels.

By 1960 the rest of the world was waking up to his efforts, and the qualities of Grange were becoming evident as the wine matured. Max and his wine received critical acclaim from those who really knew. Penfolds recommended production and today Grange Hermitage is regarded as 'the one true First Growth of the Southern Hemisphere'. Like all great wines it has its great years and 1955, 1962, 1971 and 1976 are notable. Since it takes at least fifteen years to reach its peak, many vintages have yet to prove their mettle, but I heard the year 1983 bandied about as being one to watch while I was there. Though not from the maestro himself who, like all great artists, holds a simple faith in the quality of all his work. He told me that as a boy it was the smell of the spent grape skins after distillation that first aroused his interest in wine. He was given over to a wine chemist at Penfolds when he left school during the depression in 1931 as a fetch-and-carry boy. The chemist taught him basic testing procedures.

He studied chemistry and did a lot of experimental work on the various wine bacteria diseases, but it wasn't until the harnessing of the pH factor that bacterial infection could be controlled. He was the first in the area to use pH theory to maintain levels of acidity, sulphur and alcohol above those at which bacteria thrive. Max Schubert has no time for rule-of-thumb methods, though he acknowledges that in Europe ideal climatic conditions make the process less critical. He claims that you cannot make wine in Southern Australia without the means to control temperature.

'Half the time grape material reaches the crusher from vineyards out here at temperatures which are far too hot to make good wine. When you take into consideration that for every degree of sugar fermenting you have an increase in heat of some three degrees your wine is going to be finished before it even starts fermenting. It attracts bacteria of all kinds, and other extraneous matter—all the materials, in fact, to make a very bad wine.'

Coonawarra Railway Station

Peter Douglas, Winemaker, Wynns (Penfolds) Coonawarra

Coonawarra wines have good longevity but they don't reward cellaring. They don't improve. If anything, they peak and stay on the plateau for a number of years and then slowly go quite bitter with a grainy aftertaste.

When I leave Coonawarra I represent Coonawarra first and then Penfolds second. The biggest word on the label becomes Coonawarra. Therefore it must be bloody good. We are such a small community that we can't afford to wrangle. We socialise. We live together; it's not one château versus the next château.

I think the good bit is just about to happen. A lot of people will mention in one breath something like Pétrus and Lindemans, or Château Latour and Wynns Coonawarra Estate, and that's when everyone in Coonawarra will be a lot happier. I guess it's what generates all our energies.

When you're standing there, working really hard, producing some damn fine wines and you find these other people hanging on to a reputation that's already 200 years old and getting ten times as much for their wines as we are, it's hard to swallow. Yet if you had them blind in a tasting, nine times out of ten our wines come out on top.

Ian Huntley, Export Director, Penfolds

The Barossa Valley is still the centre of the Lutheran Church in Australia and the missionaries that went to New Guinea all came from around here. [Pause] They drink Koonunga Hill in Canterbury nowadays. Our agent said a gentleman was at their office on Saturday morning and he ordered about 50 cases of Koonunga Hill. He paid for it from the Archbishop of Canterbury's account.

Dr Christopher Rawson Penfold

Penfold's 1985 Bin 222, Eden Valley Cabernet Sauvignon This is a wine to decant. A slow, rock-steady pouring against the light ensures that the crusty sediment in the wine can be kept in the bottle at the neck and not allowed to mix with the decanted wine. When you return the bottle to the upright position you can see the sediment sliding back down the inside. Nothing wrong here. Just an indication of the extract, tannins and tartrates allowed to remain in the bottle which help to retain flavour. Decanting also allows such a full bodied *wunderkind* to breathe for a while. The hairs on your chest sprout secondary shoots as Dr Penfold intended. The colour is a warm brownish-red. Rich, thick and woody, it complements the marinated and braised haunch of a well-sprung common kangaroo.

Wynns 1982 John Riddoch Cabernet Sauvignon This was the first vintage of Wynns John Riddoch. A massive body—it swells to gargantuan proportions—the primal savage emerges—thunder in the brain. Time opens its doors and you come face to face with immortality.

John Riddoch

Max Schubert, Wine Supremo, Magill Estate, Grange Hermitage

We don't make French wines. We make Australian wines. We can never make a French wine of any description but we can make a damn good Australian wine.

You know there's no treatment works for effluent in the cellars. So it has to be done by evaporation. It smells in the air quite close to the cellars. We had a duck and it was there for three or four years and it was constantly drunk. The air was so smelly it wouldn't move; it loved it.

When Max first made his leap of faith in 1951 to create an entirely new wine to last a minimum of 20 years, such a thing was unheard of. Nobody in their right mind would do that to a table wine. Max did it and proved his point. With a touch of madness common to all genius, he created a classic upon which the whole Australian industry measures its quality.

Australia's success story speaks for itself. Its greatest wines bear comparison with those from any other continent, while satisfying their own bench mark of excellence. Australians are master winemakers now and wine is as much a part of their souls as any art form.

However, what crossed my mind while being shown such expertise, was the realisation that so

Wynns' Winery, Coonawarra Estate

many of these enterprises were started by diggers, wheat growers, drovers, cattle farmers, convicts and other gold-crazed hopefuls, and for every one of them who made it work, a thousand failed for a thousand reasons, from drought to rank incompetence.

It is to those brave souls, those disappointed Bazzas of long ago that I take my cabbage-tree hat off and I honour a few of them here. Nothing so good as Australian wine ever developed without some pain.

There's CAPTAIN RACE PEUGEOT who lingered too long in port and after a promising start ended his days trying to market wombat furs.

'WOGGA' STAINES, who planted too many Semillon grapes and had no means of cooling his wines. 'WARM WOGGA WHITE' became a byword for urine and Wogga died a disappointed connoisseur.

BRINDELL PACKSTAFF, an ex-convict, gained his freedom welshing on his mates. He cheated a tribe of Aboriginals out of 2,000 square miles of bush country to grow Shiraz. He became the vinegar king of Adelaide, but died lonely.

Aussie in Bazzas Smokin' Great Barrier Reefer.

'DIGEREE' TENTERDEN thought he had it made with TENTERDEN'S FORTIFIED BOGGO but, like so many others before him and since, he misjudged the new Australian appetite for wine as something akin to SNAKE BITE. He cut off the top of his hat and went mad in the sun.

BRICE GUMSTUCK grabbed the headlines in the YANCO GLEN EXAMINER with his revolutionary winemaking process. He found that half a pint of CASSOWARY SPIT added to each thousand gallons of GUMSTUCK FLAT RED made wine brewed in cattle troughs taste OAK MATURED and NUTTY. When the YANCO locals sprouted blue feathers and head-lumps it was all traced back to GUMSTUCK's process. He became YANCO's first mayor and lived to be 110.

RED ROD CARSTAIRS and his little companion, PINKY FLOWERMOUNT, came hand in hand among the cattle drovers winning wide respect for their ROSE PETAL wine and MINT TEA served from a bullock cart. They put down roots at TONGO and grew grapes for the FRUIT TRADE and the OPAL miners. They would crush the grapes together in a large bathtub, stark naked, and for years produced a

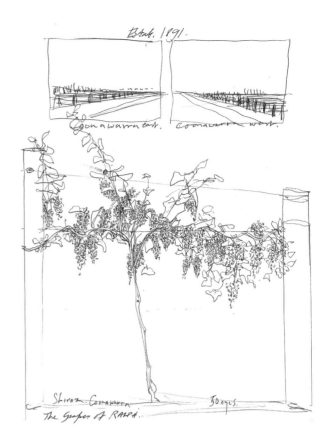

Coonawarra EAST

brutal little vintage called MOTHER'S MILK. Both were drowned at work.

FATHER MALLORY O'FEELY nurtured his widely scattered flock of diggers and CATTLE DROVERS with a fortified brew he aged in empty coffins behind his little bush church in COONGOLA. Having nailed the coffin lid in place during fermentation, he would often become confused and bury it with a full service and last rites. Never a businessman, O'FEELY's winemaking remained a spiritual endeavour though he never gave up his love of it.

Little is known of BRUCE GUTTERIDGE III, except that his '99 end of century POONCARLE HERMITAGE was the end of him and the beginning of wine control. He was last heard of in the GREY RANGE town of BULGROO, peddling BULGROO BUGWASH next to his wine vat—an ABORIGINAL WATERHOLE which he filled with STRINGBARK and SCORPION TEARS. Drovers used to make a detour over STURTS STONY DESERT rather than pass through BULGROO.

The driving force behind many of the men were, of course the women with spirits as tough as mulga scrub who survived like swamp fever in the monsoon season. Such women as:

Little FANNY BUCHANAN, 'the girl with the cattle-prod eyes', who helped her husband to concoct BOTRYTIS RED ROT to sell at the Immigrant Reception Depot at Murrumburrah. Upwardly mobile new Australians spurned it as a drink to forget. Little Fanny's husband, STUMPY, hung himself from a dead gum, and FANNY lived on to emulate his example as the worst winemaker south of DUBBO CREEK. She made a fortune out of DEAD MAN'S GULCH, a paint stripper of a brew made from BOILED PLATYPUS SKINS and IRON FILINGS.

BIG DOLLY FRINTON pursued her husband right up to NORTH QUEENSLAND and got him making wine out of dusty MULGA, GIDGEE and BRIGALOW SCRUB. The taste was too radical even for the Australian palate, more used to the broader dimensions offered by MASTICATED TREE BARK.

MABLE McCUBBERY: her husband made his name as the TOWANG FLOGGER, handing out corporal punishment across the backs of chain gangs at the TOWANG stockade, south of GOULBURN. He did the same to his vines and produced a rare vintage. Unfortunately he went soft and lost his touch. MABLE never had it.

awarra WEST.

Ralph STEADman 89

Mechanical Harvesting *Ralph Steadman '89*

BAROSSA PEARL ran a Catholic soup kitchen for down-and-out GOLD PROSPECTORS while her husband, Archbishop CONNEMARA, a BENEDICTINE, roamed the outback on horseback preaching the evils of abstinence and administering communion wine as an answer to everything from DINGO BITE to DAMNATION.

'LONG FLAT RED', as she was known, dyed all her dresses in her husband's vintage of '94. He, 'CUBBY' GALWAY, sunk his gold into a 50-mile stretch of the HUNTER Valley which ultimately became a road. Nothing grew after the first year of '94. LONG FLAT buried him in one of her dresses.

GRANDMA SKEHAN joined her husband, BANDY, after a lifetime of Irish waiting, when he finally gave up GOLD prospecting and planted vines on a patch of scrub he was given following the FREE SELECTION ACT which effectively wrested land from the powerful squatter LAND KINGS. BANDY'S VINES turned out to be POISONBUSH and he was prosecuted on a charge of mass manslaughter.

WINDY WENDY McCLAVITEE, so named as the widow of WHISPERING McCLAVITEE whose sparkling white wine was so gassy it blew his customers into the outback on their way through PENOLA where they ran a POSTHOUSE vineyard. WHISPERING McCLAVITEE exploded during a special turn-of-the-century tasting of NANGWARRY.

It was on a trip to Australia's cultural heartland of Alice Springs and Ayers Rock when the uncomfortable feeling crept up on me that the plight of the Aboriginal is more desperate than I ever realised. There you see the results of Whitey's taming of the most antediluvian landmass in the world. The fact is he hasn't tamed it but he's left some pitiful human debris around in the process of trying.

He has done his best to make it fit for Whitey to live in but, in typical colonial style, he hasn't done much for the continent's true inheritors. The stumbling trickle of humanity that wandered the streets of their own back yard made me feel ashamed. It made the primary reason for my visit rather incongruous. But maybe if I hadn't come for the primary reason I wouldn't have become aware of the second one.

Back along the coastal grazing lands and sugar plantations around Townsville we came across the remains of a stronger reason why Whitey suffered so readily to make his mark on a thankless environment. Ravenswood was a shell of a place littered with the remains of gold-mining machinery, where street shop fronts and wooden hotels would mushroom overnight and just as soon be sawn away and moved on to wherever someone shouted 'GOLD!'. In what was left of the place you could almost feel the fever in the air. So potent had been the lure to desperate men that its power had threatened the very fabric of an emerging nation.

Wine is a gentler way to find gold and maybe the gentler temperaments of the men who make it can find a way to help the Aborigines, even though the Aborigine can never drink their product. Somewhere in there is the irony and maybe in the irony is the solution. Many wines at least proudly sport strong Aboriginal names on their labels, without prejudice.

Perhaps without prejudice these prosperous men can divert some of that prosperity to help the very race they honour through their wines.

[In the cooper's shop]
We don't have any Irish among us do we? That's alright. This is what a cooper calls an Irish nail. It's not hard to see why. It's got two points. We've even got a thing called Irish putty. Ordinary reeds from the river. You shouldn't have to use them if a job's done properly. If you machine your joints properly a barrel won't leak.

THE TEN COMMANDMENTS OF WINE

1 Thou shalt not bad-mouth a winegrower in his own region.

2 Thou shalt not pick any grapes but thine own.

3 Thou shalt not grow any grapes but approved varieties.

4 Thou shalt not take the names of the Grands Crus in vain.

5 Eight days shalt thou labour, and on the ninth may come a frost but that's OK.

6 Honour thy critics that they shall know best and put thee out of business.

7 Thou shalt not kill them in spite of their presumptions. They are but human yet their job is holy.

8 Thou shalt not commit adulterous vintage-enhancing post-fermentation tricks.

9 Thou shalt not steal a Gold Medal. Thy wine will give thee away sooner or later.

10 Thou shalt not bear false witness against thy nearest rival nor laugh at the shape of his spiffy new designer bottle.

11 Well, that's ten, but thou shalt not covet thy neighbour's new high-tech fermentation vat, nor his new oak barrels either, nor his bottling line, nor even his new big deal to supply a supermarket chain worldwide. Thou shalt make do with coveting his wife.

Our visit to Coonawarra was a mixture of pain and pleasure. Pain, because I got sick on Sydney prawns which had been quietly awaiting my arrival on the Sunday evening. They began to lay me low at exactly the time on Monday morning when we had to travel to Sydney, Melbourne, Portland and Mt Gambier. A kind local taxied us to the Mt Gambier clinic where I was injected with Maxalon (Bin 989) to suppress nausea, but no treatment for the actual cause of the problem. We drove about 50 km by taxi to our hosts at the Chardonnay Hotel, my head resting pathetically on Anna's lap on the back seat.

I felt wretched. When we arrived I was in no condition to sign in and immediately climbed into bed in our chalet-type room, mountain-style bare bricks and natural wood beams. I needed a doctor. The nearest one, at Penola, a town 8 km away, could not come out to me. I had to be driven. We waited over an hour. I slept in the stiff seated position and woke with a jolt as my face hit the head rest of the front seat. In the surgery, a lady entered and asked if any of us had a cold virus. I told her I had at least one, probably English, and possibly an army of Old World infections on the march, looking for fresh fields to conquer. As she backed away the doctor's door opened and she disappeared before we had a chance to say it was our turn.

When I did finally get in the surgery I had self-cured marginally as one does in the presence of a doctor who is wearing shorts, open-necked short-sleeved shirt and full length white socks. He diagnosed gastro-enteritis—blood pressure 160 over 100, far too high—and take these pills, no alcohol, just water, flat lemonade, dry toast for eats. Hopefully it'll be a 24-hour wonder. I didn't dare argue. A man is a wimp in these parts getting sick on prawns and showing it. A few tubes of Fosters and a quick chunder behind a gum tree is the usual remedy and no questions asked, mate.

Eighteen hours later, I had to face up to Penfolds 1985 Cabernet Sauvignon, Bin 707. We were

The First Fermentation Smelling Ceremony

sitting in what was once a shepherd's cottage and the first building to be erected in 1851. The small oak-beamed room was filled by a square table which had just enough space for its seated eaters and a passage for the cook, proprietor and well-mannered wine pourer France to circulate with the tucker and booze. Though the food bordered on Nouvelle Cuisine, it had the Maître's own Austrian character (he used to be chef to the King and Queen of the Netherlands), and this helped a wine of pernicious brilliance to soften on the tongue and caress a beleaguered liver and ravaged stomach into comfortable submission. Wines of this quality are dangerously good at turning the most sophisticated imbiber into a 40-cent wino over a relatively short period of time. It's definitely a, 'well, let's-have-another-bottle-of-this' kind of wine.

Wine BATS over the BAROSSA VALLEY

Ralph STEADman

PENFOLD'S annual wine making FRENZY.
NURIOOTPA. March 1989

The Chancellor of the Wine Guild Lord Montagu — a broker of Wine Experts.

English Wine Conversation

Man A: Cha'eau PLONK! That's the stuff, mate. I dunno the difference, anyway. It's all baloney, in' it? You wouldn't catch me spittin' it aht. What they bleedin' fink it is, marfwash?? All them nobs suckin' and blowin' with a la de dah accent—makes yer sick. Well, I frow it up anyway. Anything foreign. Part of the pleasure. What? I like a nice pint—like the next plonker—anytime of the day or night. It's our drink, in' it? But them geezers wiv all that crap abaht aromas an' bodies an' noses . . . Then they bring it to yer in a basket—I don't mind a chicken in a basket—but a bottle of bloody plonk on its side, mate—that's empty, s'far as I'm concerned. Wankers. Don't know what they're talkin' abaht, most of 'em. One or two maybe. Them experts—they know a fing or two, but it ain't nuffin' t'do wiv me.

Man with La De Dah Accent: I think you are missing the point, old chap. There is simply nothing to compare with Oysters Feuilletée in a light sauce of oyster juice, wine and butter complemented by a bottle of, say, Château Malartic-Lagravière from the Graves region of the Bordeaux—probably an '82. Absolute heaven. Then, perhaps, a filo pastry stuffed with asparagus and leek to clean the palate before the main course—with a Ladoucette Pouilly-Fumé: simply delicious. And then you are ready for the rack of venison in a wine sauce and a big, full-bodied burgundy, your first bottle of Chambertin-Clos de Bèze perhaps—a favourite of Napoleon's, incidentally. Two bottles of that to help cut a swathe through the cheese board, et voilà! The chilled Grand Marnier Soufflé will arrive before you can say Muscat de Beaumes-de-Venise, Domaine de Coyeux 1986, for the classic finale. Then pamper yourself with a few glasses of Graham's 1977 Vintage Port. Now that's what I call a breakfast and if you are feeling queasy, have the Billecart-Salmon Champagne to start, with your oysters. Works like a rocket through yer bowels.

A: Winkles.

Man with the La De Dah Accent: I beg your pardon?

A: Winkles, mate. I'll have the winkles to start. Followed by jellied eels, a couple of pints of Old Peculier. Wash it down, clean the marf out like. Then a dollop of steak-and-kidney pud off that trolley wiv some of that red body plonk you went on abaht. Napoleon's wallop, I fink you said, and plenty of Wuster sauce, peas an' mash. I won't 'ave the cheese, mate. Gives me gip. I'll 'ave the puddin'! Spotted dick and trifle—you can put the port in that. Luvley! An' if you wanna spoil me, get us a couple o' bottles of Newcastle Brarn and I'll join 'er as you drink yer port.

Man with the La De Dah Accent: Very well, Kev, but I think you are making a big mistake.

A: Yeah, big mistake. The workin' classes made a big mistake lettin' you posh geezers get away wiv murder for so long. Anyway, up yours, mate. You're a toff. Here's to you. Let's 'ave annuvver while we're waitin'. What did yer say yer do fer a livin'?

Man with the La De Dah Accent: I'm a plasterer with Bubbly Buffy St John Babbington who runs a vineyard at Bumshot Manor. You should try his HEXELREBE Dry White. But then you would probably like his BOGSDOWN SEYVAL BLANC with your preference for Newcastle Brown. I did hear that Buffy was thinking about creating a communion sparkling wine for the Bishop from a Müller-Thurgau blended with Madeleine Angevine. The Bishop prefers a white himself and he blessed Buffy's first vintage back in 1977. Personally, I can't wait to try his first ever English bubbly made with Chardonnay grapes. He's calling it GRAND BRUTAGNE SPITLERS PING to appeal to the home market. It has a certain zest to it, don't you think? Do you, er, like champagne?

Kev: I don't remember. Last time I 'ad it was at me muvver's funeral, an' I passed arht after free bottles. Me mum always liked a nice drop of stout wiv a gin chaser. Kept 'er goin' for years, that did. She never went near champagne. It always said BRUT on the bottle and she fort it was fizzy after-shave.

Man with the La De Dah Accent: What do *you* do, Kev, for a living?

Kev: I work for Suvverby's, don't I?

Man with the La De Dah Accent: Oh really, I say. Er—haulage?

Kev: Nah, mate. Corkage. Sniffer in the English Wine Department. Just started up. Quali'y control y' know. Gotta watch out for all them additives. Bloody wevver, see. The grapes don't ripen like they do on the con-ee-nont. You'd be amazed how many people use rhubarb to increase the acidity. Gives the wine longevity, see. Notalot of people know that.

Man with the La de Dah Accent: I had no idea—.

Kev: Neever would yer. It's me nose, see. Perfick for the job. I was born in Billingsgate—got perfick pitch. Some people use rhubarb; uvvers try a bit of beetroot and call it red. Best red I ever saw—a Cabernet Pinot Noir—looked beautiful! FORTY FAR-SAND LITRES!! Couldn't believe it. Someink wrong 'ere, I fawt. I sniffed it for days. I nearly got the sack, 'cos they was aucshun it orf, weren't they? Wednesday mornin'. Lincolnshire Bloodbarf, they called it. 1976. Bit early, see. Suspicious. Bloody impossible, in fact. Punters were swarmin' ararnd on the Tuesdee. Bloody excitement, never seen anyfink like it. Some country nob sniffed it first and knew there was summink queer goin' on. Giv it to me, didn' 'e? Then fretenned me wiv re-dundancy. So I sniffed it like a Baskerville blood'ound. What do you fink?

Man with the La De Dah Accent: I have absolutely *no* idea. I'm riveted!

Kev: Elderberry, mate. England's great burgundy! Always was. But it's the iron wot dun it. Château Cortina, I call it! More iron in elderberry than a junk yard full of secon'and cars. Never learn, that lot. Couldn't disguise a smell like that wiv a lemon meringue.

Man with the La De Dah Accent: Good gracious! What happened?

Kev: Well, they poured it darn the sink, didn' they? Made it rare. Rarity becomes the vintage attraction, dunnit? Blamed it on the late frost. That's wot they trade on. How d'yer fink Bordeaux gets by? Keep it rare. Blame it on the frost. Happens every year. If they don't 'ave a late frost, they 'ave 'umidity. In August. Mildew. Gotta blame summink. Uvverwise, there's more grapes than you would need to make a tidal wave. Wine lakes everywhere. Not enough people in the world to drink it, see. They bring in all these geezers to sniff abaht the place and give it a pedigree—but when it comes darn to it, they're tryin' to make summink precious outa summink common. And the guvverment's involved.

Man with the La De Dah Accent: You don't mean the Government?

Kev: The Guvverment. All them duties, see. Keep it goin', they say—an' start an anti-drink cam-paign for Christmas. Well, that's the problem, in'it? Drink quali'y, mate—that's wot they say, but don't drink. Problem is, after the first two bottles, anyfink goes. And the next thing you know, yer blowin' in a bag on the M25. It's all wrong. Yer average geezer don't know the differ-ence. Wiv Newcastle Brarn, you know what to do wiv it. Frow it up and get home in one piece. Drink's not for keeping mate, not even in a cellar. But they never learn, do they? That's wot Suvverby's trades on. Not drinkin' it. Lay it on its side—and invite yer friends to look at it.

Go forth—happy that we have judged you

Ralph's Vineyard Diary

While on location in northern Italy for the Oddbins Italian list, in February 1990, I met a winemaker called Luigi Ferrando who showed us his wine cellar in the old Roman town of Carema, nestling comfortably in the lower slopes of the Alps. It was a magical little place crowded with oak and cherrywood barrels, a stainless-steel vat and a one-bar electric fire warming a late fermentation.

Adjoining his cellar was a quaint little room looking down into the valley. The emphasis on 'little' characterised the whole operation. An oil-cloth-covered table stood in the middle of the floor with four chairs, and around the walls were racked wines going back to the late '60s, in red earthenware wine racks, displayed with a modest pride. Ferrando gave us a tasting of the last five vintages of his Carema, made from the Piedmontese grape Nebbiolo, and it all made perfect sense. *It was at that moment I resolved to create my own vineyard.*

In early March 1990, I contacted David Shaw, vineyard consultant at Nutbourne Manor Vineyard and a colleague of Christopher (Kit) Lindlar, winemaker for a whole army of winegrowers in the southeast of England. His winery is at Grafty Green in Kent.

I made my first appointment with Kit as soon as possible and, on 13th March 1990, Gordon Kerr and I set off to see him. This was a more difficult task than I had first thought, because Grafty Green has a habit of not being where you think it is. It changes location as though it has a haunted will of its own.

We found the winery after a process of elimination and *déjà vu* detours through winding lanes and mud. It looked the antithesis of anything we had seen in the rest of Europe if only for the remoteness of its setting and the sense of abandonement. Old Nissen-style hangars, grey asbestos and deserted dreams of years ago sat hunkered down like old-age pensioners in their favourite seats.

At the back of all this desolation we found a newish doorway, the entrance proper to High Weald Winery. We met Kit Lindlar who struck me as a kind of male Joyce Grenfell. He seemed, to judge by his surprise, to have forgotten we were expected, or maybe nobody ever keeps their word in the wine business.

We had imagined a hive of industry. He had told me on the phone that bottling was in progress, but the bottling plant had broken down and he was alone. The really great surprise was the plant itself—the hub of his industry and I suspect the centre of his life. An impressive display of new German fermentation vats enclosed in an old hanger looked as serious as anything we had seen, though on a smaller scale.

We were given a tasting of the 1989 Bacchus white, an aggressive but very fruity creation, straight from the vat, and the wholly more subtle Schönburger, a surprising wine which developed its body and structure far later in the tasting. Its fragrance lingered and I found great enjoyment in its character. Then came the rather pleasant moment of choosing vinestocks from a list of a dozen varieties. I took 50 Schönburgers and 50 of the German Spätburgunder (Pinot Noir), from which most winegrowers at present would run a mile, not wanting to risk no crop or a mean crop.

After a delivery time of three weeks I received my vines. I was on the way to realising my ambition to have my own vineyard and maybe one day declare a vintage alonside the best of them. Château Loose, Appellation L'Alerte Rouge, was but a dream away.

5th April 1990

I am still awaiting the delivery of my vines. Kit Lindlar has been in Germany, but he is expected back in England today or tomorrow, depending on the Customs men. I ask Sid (my part-time gardener) to dig me a shallow trough in the shade to accommodate the vines and keep their roots damp while I prepare each one individually.

I am informed that the vine suppliers, Steinmann Reben, ship their vines prepared and paraffin-waxed ready to plant, so the axial shoots should already be pruned. I have to avoid using compost or peat fertilizer to prevent any scorching of the tender young shoots. I also have to be careful with watering: waterlogging is a dangerous condition for vines. The last two days have brought five-degree frosts, so I hope that we do not get this again during planting.

7th April 1990

I get a call on my answerphone that the vines had arrived and that I could collect them any time. On the same tape was a call from my friend Tim Doust who had missed me by 30 seconds at the pub. Could he see me? 'Come up' I phoned back, and we toasted the idea of collecting 100 vines with a

Guinness and Scotch chaser. Just one, since we had to drive to collect.

It is a sunny day and we drive with the hood down, bringing a blast of genuine pleasure on the open road. Grafty Green is hard to find but now, after three visits, I had cracked the code. Kit Lindlar met us and, with not too much preamble, presented me with a polythene bag the size of a laundry basket containing 100 vines. I received yet another set of instructions and we were off—playing Rolling Stones' 'Steel Wheels' all the way back. Now I knew it was serious. One packet of 100 dependent little lives—mine to nurture and grow.

The trench Sid had dug proved ample to lay out the rootstock vines, each with its bunch of roots like Rastafarian dreadlocks. I covered the roots gently and watered them.

I felt that the solemnity of the moment required something symbolic with which to celebrate, so I opened a bottle of Luigi Ferrando's Carema 1983 to toast and welcome the vines as they lay temporarily in their shallow trough.

The tops of the vines were crowned with stumps and lumps and green paraffin wax to reduce the weeping that follows severe pruning. They lay there like bronze maquettes waiting to be transformed into full-sized monuments to their own potential.

Tim and I toasted the vines well—pouring wine on to a spade and scattering it about on to the soil in ritual solemnity. The sun was turning west and shadows were lengthening over the vines, which no doubt expected yet another unknown shock. No such thing. They were now cossetted, awaiting careful planting. Their new home, however, had to be geometrically marked out. What you plan is what you reap.

In the light of the waxing moon, over the tips of the waxed plantings, I toasted the vines yet again and blessed them as before, casting a bottle of Bulgarian Pinot Noir over the new vineyard with the utmost abandon. I bade them good night and retired, spending some of the small hours in anxious action-replay of the mind, adjusting, lining up, even completing the task of planting 100 vines. I slept at last and rose at 7.30. We were expecting friends at noon.

8th April 1990
I resolved to go out first thing and buy the sharpest secateurs, a smaller spade and 100 canes to mark out the plot.

On my return our guests, Gary and Sandy Day Ellison, had arrived. Since they were both graphic designers and art directors, I could not have wished for a sharper and more suitable couple to help me measure out the geometric perfection of God's earth in a chosen spot.

We spent the afternoon in vigorous deliberation, establishing, marking, adjusting, re-adjusting and marking again the exact spot where each plant was to live. You cannot plant a single vine until you are certain that where you plant it is within an inch of being the exact spot in which the vine should be for posterity—to provide the anchor and linchpin of everything that comes after. You can never replant. Nor must it be taken for granted that your plot has a single square corner or level on it. God's earth defies our perception of horizontal, vertical, straight or even cock-eyed.

The earth deceives our senses and we should bow to its great and complex idiosyncracies. However, once a corner has been established it should be believed in and protected against all other well-meaning suggestions, otherwise a prospective winegrower's sanity is at risk.

We moved the centre of my vineyard nearer to the high south-facing wall than I had originally intended, to capture the warmest rays of the sun for most of the day. There is also a high terraced rise of old stones and soil up against the wall and I am tempted to try five vines along it to gain the benefit of height and trapped sun—not to mention the aggressive rubble inside it, which must surely be good for the vines' root struggle.

The great sense of order our guests possessed in their capacity as designers kept my maniacal enthusiasm in check and probably prevented a serious error of judgement on my part, on account of natural passion for the job in hand.

So, to date, there are three patron saints of my vineyard—St Tim, St Gary and Santa Maria Sandy. Their help at those vital early stages may well prove to be seminal to the success of my venture. They will be rewarded. Each will be allotted a vine on a spot within the vineyard which will be forever theirs. A symbol will mark them out for their own inspection—and the inspection of posterity. QUOTE: They shall not die, but live forever in our hearts and on our palates!

The canes are in the earth, set firm until each vine is established at that very point. At least there exists on the earth's turgid surface a tiny island of order and endeavour sufficient to defy the vagaries of modern life—without being reactionary. This is a haven of passion, after all. Passion for the grape and passion for what it can produce. What is endeavour if it is not driven by a passion born of conviction, and the belief that anything to do with art needs an artist to guide its destiny? I offer myself as an artist who will willingly give these sibling roots all the attention they deserve to bring them to fruition.

10th April 1990

With Derek HOAD, St Derek of the vineyard as he now is, I set about planting one hundred vines, 50 red and 50 white. Each vine must be set in the soil 12–15 inches (30.5–38 cm) deep. That's about a 125-foot (38-metre) hole if you were digging all in the same place. Beginning was an anxious experience. Would I lay the roots out as the text book demands? And, worse, I had to cut off the roots' tenuous fingers to 3½ (9 cm) inches—the width of a man's hand. Would they die? What if they all die because I acted on a misprint in the instructions? What responsibility! What carnage! Planting my first vine was fraught with such misgivings. I pleaded with my vines to forgive me and trust my intuition as an artist and a surgeon.

The first three holes were reasonably easy to dig, according to St Derek of the Vineyard who dug them—I was a better, perhaps more sensitive planter who could arrange the roots as is required around a small mound of soft earth at the bottom of the hole. The arrangement worked wonderfully. St Derek is a natural hole-digger whose technique betrays previous training as a Maidstone Council gravedigger.

Several holes later hinted that perhaps it would not all be plain sailing. We hit some kind of cobbled ragstone left buried from the time when the whole site had been a barn and stables. Some holes seemed to coincide with huge slabs of stone which had to be cajoled out of their resting place with crowbars. Suddenly, there was nothing but soil and the job progressed apace.

Ten plants later, I was becoming expert in judging the cutting of roots and the umbrella-like arrangement of the roots over a mound of soil in the bottom of the hole, then the gentle covering of the roots with soft soil. Finally the height check of the graft cluster above the surface of the soil was made easier by using a 2-inch (5-cm) wide length of wood laid across the hole before it is filled in. While there is little soil over the roots, the stock can be raised or lowered very gently to adjust the height and then filled in completely in two stages. Several inches of soil are first dropped into the hole and pressed gently, then the rest can be shovelled in to complete the job, pressed firmly 2 inches (5 cm) below the graft. The strange, incandescent, green-topped vines began to accummulate like a regiment, each vine marked also by the cane at its side. Some of the vines reminded me of sea horses' heads.

On the first day we managed to plant 51 vines which got us over the psychological hump. I gave the first day's work a thorough watering and blessed them with Guinness.

April 11th 1990

Another pleasant day—no rain. Started work at 9.30 a.m. We soon found difficult problems with rocks. If Robert Doutres (see page 12) is right, then some rock around the root system causes the vine to fight and thrive with more resilience. A vine is, in a sense, a weed which grows best in rough rocky areas. Provided it has some soil around the roots to get it going then it will fight its way through the toughest underground conditions. This fight builds character.

We finished the planting of 98 of the vines by 5.50 p.m. and completed the area of 9 rows by 11 (99 vines) with two white Schönburgers to spare. I got a free one! I decided to try the experiment I had been thinking about earlier and planted the remaining two on the rocky soil up against the wall. I now have a vineyard—a real live vineyard, and the next weeks will be a time of suspense as I wait to see if the vines survive and flourish.

April 12th 1990

Sid, the gardener, arrived and surveyed the new plantation of vines with a certain scepticism. Not that he doesn't think it's a good idea; but he's not sure of this new experience of keeping an eye on such a serious crop. I was nervous when I planted the first vine, but I feel a sense of achievement about just getting these hardy little beggars into the soil. It was like a rescue operation in a way, reducing the time these refugees would be in transit and getting them into a home of their own.

There are two beautiful small elms (self-seeded) at the top of the new vineyard slope close to the wall. Though casting some shade over the vines, their bright new yellow-green leaves create an enchanting dapple.

Because the wall has a slight tilt to it which might produce a problem later, I discussed with St Derek the possibility of building two small shrines (as they have in many French vineyards) against the wall to act as buttresses to check any further tilt—and also, as shrines, to bless, protect and

encourage the vineyard. Within each shrine, St Derek will build a recess large enough to place a bottle of fine white wine in one and a bottle of fine red in the other, just to remind the thrusting little souls just what the hell they are there for, when the fruit begins to form. A future task . . .

April 13th 1990

The rain in the night amounted to nothing but the morning still looks grey and threatening. By 11 a.m. it just threw it down and thus, in my opinion, the gods blessed my little vineyard, ensuring a promising start and a stronger future. I looked at the green paraffin wax, earnestly searching for signs of life. After the rain finished, the sun shone through a piece of flaky wax and I thought for a moment that I saw something move. It was nothing, though. It was just the breeze caressing loose wax.

April 17th 1990

Today the *Daily Mail* announced that English wine production has gone up to massive levels. The EC now declares England a wine-producing nation and votes to clap controls on us like putting rocks around a swimmer's ankles, allowing only certain grape varieties as acceptable for wine production.

April 20th 1990

We have been having plenty of rain to bed in the vines—they have been well blessed. Any time now the buds will begin to pop. Derek has begun to build the Wine Vine Shrine as a buttress to hold up the main wall. The posts for the trellising are now installed, so it's beginning to look like a vineyard.

April 23rd 1990

Wrote to the MD of Oddbins, Derek Morrison, and

invited him to be a Saint of the Vineyard. I suppose I should also ask my agent, Abner Stein; St Abner could then take his commission in wine. The weather has turned a little milder and more springlike—the late frost killed off the wisteria's and the walnut tree's first budding. Wisterias often come again, but the walnut is a strange and brooding tree. I may have to beat it with a big stick.

April 25th 1990

More rain: good good good.

April 30th 1990

Inspected the vines and found the buds beginning to break. I have started rubbing out the excess buds, so that one will rise from the scion and become the main rootstock stem.

May 7th 1990

The vines are making excellent progress. Only one is still refusing to show its face; 100 out of 101 have taken. There is still a chance of late frost so I resist rubbing out extraneous buds.

May 10th 1990

Rain is in short supply: we've been having really dry weather. Luckily the vines will be well watered in from the last fall of rain and from my hosepipe watering—but by Saturday a hosepipe ban will be in force.

May 17th 1990

Scottish film crew arrived to film me giving my 'gardening hints' and talking about my vineyard for a new-style gardening programme called 'DIG'. It was a perfect day and everything went well— even the controlled explosion technique I employ to spread compost, shift winter turnips and blow next door's cat back over the wall where it belongs. I spoke of the 'spirituality' of growing vines and the lack of soul in much of the wine scene. Not a job for accountants. The vines are really breaking out now though there's still no sign of life in the lonely one. The 'shrines' are finished and look fabulous.

May 20th 1990

Rubbed out the excess buds today, leaving just two or three until I am certain which is the best, most upright bud to become the main stock.

May 22nd 1990

The vines are pushing out hard—except the one

that has still not taken. I rub out the extra buds popping out all over the junctions of the main stock and scion just above the graft.

May 23rd 1990
St Derek, who has done a wonderful job on the shrines, has begun to build a ruined wall which will have a slab table at its end jutting out as a buttress—both decorative and functional. There is quite an atmosphere at the top of the vineyard now, a strong aesthetic presence.

May 25th 1990
Today comes a delightful surprise. The last vine, the one that I thought hadn't made it, has struck. A pink ripple of a bud pushes through the wax.

The drought continues. I bought a small submersible pump and sunk it into the well behind the house. I was hoping it was a spring well but I fear it is only a rain collector of limited capacity.

May 26th 1990
A Penfolds wine man, Ian Huntley, arrives, and is very impressed by my vineyard. The weather is still dry and a strange cool wind is blowing from the east.

May 29th 1990
The last vine to bud is still growing, while the rest of the vines are shooting up. The top end of the vineyard is looking really atmospheric as Derek (Saint) puts the finishing touches to the cast concrete table top, for wine tastings in years to come. It was Anna's idea; she's a clever thing.

I will soon need to tie the growing shoots to their bamboo canes. Still no rain and the rainwell is now empty. I am looking for other underground chambers to conserve what we can when we can—not a particularly British habit since rainwater was never in short supply before the climatic changes we are now experiencing.

May 31st 1990
The vineyard is looking greener, despite there being still no rain. Elsewhere in the garden, things look yellow.

June 1st 1990
Today, it rained! and gave the garden a good soaking—though not enough yet for real benefit.

June 3rd 1990
It didn't rain—though it tried to. The vines are still pushing on well.

Gillian Pearkes, in her book *Winegrowing in Britain,* suggests a first-year spray with sulphur and a zinc product called Zineb. I am not too keen on her suggestions. She advocates too many chemicals too soon and I would prefer to hold off this first year. I remember a word of warning from Nicolas Joly from the Loire region of France who spurned all chemicals as 'agents to denature the soil', rendering it chemically neutralised. He may be right. Industrially manufactured insecticides and fungicides will ultimately upset a natural ecological balance by destroying both pests and predators.

Chemicals like sulphur and potash and copper should be safe and sufficient. I wonder if there would be any use in growing other plants between the rows, something which will ward off vine problems by their very presence? Something like hyssop or garlic. I am particularly interested in the theory of introducing certain predator insects into the vineyard which feed on pests. A spot of carnage would be good for the soil. I need to meet a friendly entomologist.

The white-wine vines seem to be springing up so much faster than the reds. Perhaps Schönburger is a more vigorous plant than Spätburgunder.

It has been trying to rain for a week and June has not been too pleasant. Rainclouds every day but no rain—rather cool and sombre weather. The vines must soon be wired to the upright poles to support the shoots. I really never expected everything to grow so fast.

June 15th 1990
Things moved in the vineyard as Derek cleared up the top left corner and terraced the wall area around the two lone vines. It is really looking smart now. The diagonals were put in to brace the uprights at the end of each row, and stretching bolts fixed through the posts to take the wire. The vines will soon be up to the first wire. I bought various chemical products as recommended by winegrowing experts but feel that there must be a better way. These look like dangerous substances to pour on to the soil to add to an already overburdened earth. The Zineb is OK (zinc) and the wettable sulphur and even Copruky (copper), but Ambush C and Ronilan plus Elviron look positively lethal. Avoid contact with skin, wash clothes if contaminated, and so on—poor vines and poor earth. I am loathe to use them and will only do so if things get desperate. One plant only shows signs of brown rust on three leaves.

Strange—maybe too much water when I watered them in? I will consult David Shaw, the expert.

June 20th 1990

At last we have a good downpour: it galvanises the vines into action. Tendrils begin to appear which I must pluck out at this stage. The brown leaves I removed on the advice of David Shaw. He described a method of holding the leaf on the soft part of your fingers and rubbing off the leaf at the top of the stalk with the thumbnail. This way the leaf stalk will eventually drop off and leave no scar on the stem.

The vines are now up to the first wire height—two feet and growing steadily. The odd fruiting stalk appears and must be removed. The wires have now created definite rows, and the leaves have swelled with the rain to develop overall greenness. David Shaw advised against using any chemicals whatsoever in the first year. If the plants are healthy—leave them alone. Even up to the third year it is possible to avoid any pesticide programme at all, he says.

I am still thinking about growing something between the rows of vines. Pungently leaved tomatoes may be an effective deterrent to aphids, which don't like their smell. Onions might be effective—nothing seems to attack onions, they stay near the surface and don't deplete the goodness in the deeper soil.·

June 24th 1990

We've had odd rain showers, but not enough to revive the garden. The vines look perfect, though. They won't need much water for the rest of the summer.

A TV crew arrived today to film an interview with me in the vineyard for a programme called 'Human Factor'. When asked why I grow vines, I replied that I enjoy the reflective long-term acti-vity; cabbages bore me. Vines are bibilical and I can think, relax, contemplate and anticipate the future in a philosophic vein. I just can't contemplate a row of sprouts in the same way.

June 30th 1990

Brown marks keep appearing on the leaves of the vines. Reading up, I find that it might be due to a magnesium deficiency. Applying a mixture of 8 oz (249 g) magnesium sulphate to $2\frac{1}{2}$ gallons (11.36 litres) of water to the vines should help. OK. It's organic. I'll try it. The vines look so vibrant in other respects: that's the puzzle.

July 2nd 1990

I found a vine with leaf deterioration today. It looked like red spider mite damage, but there was no sign of insects, just the skeletal cobweb effect left in holes in the leaf. I have broken my resolve and sprayed with dilute solution of insect fungicide, hoping for the best. Either side of the infected vine there was no sign of trouble and everywhere else things are fine.

July 6th 1990

The vines are now well past the first wires and I am picking out secondary buds between the leaf stalk and stem to maintain a single upright shoot. I notice that if a secondary bud gets overlooked and begins to thicken it tends to bend the main stalk by thrusting it sideways.

Today we held a vine blessing party which was a huge success. There was much bacchanalian quaffing and casting of dregs between the rows. Rain threatened, but it held off until the festivities were over.

July 10th 1990

I nipped out the rest of the secondary buds today

but unfortunately took out some top shoots by mistake. It will be interesting to see how the plants grow again. I will have to choose secondary buds high up on the stem to become the main shoots.

July 13th 1990
I walked around the vineyard this morning and discovered a vine dying back.

Looking through my books I discovered it might be honey fungus which would mean digging out the vine and sterilising the soil area with Formalin. I hope it's only leaf burn. I will wait to see what happens to the other leaves on the plant just below the tip.

July 17th 1990
The vines are really looking healthy now and I keep nipping out the vine tendrils. Some vines are now up to the second wire. All the brown marks seem to have stopped spreading—maybe there had been simply too much rain in the previous weeks.

July 18th 1990
This week is very hot: up to 30°C (86°F). I have been trying to finish all the pruning before we go off to America to visit the vineyards of the Napa Valley. I am really interested in seeing more of other people's vineyards since planting my own. I hope to learn about procedure and cultivation at first hand.

July 26th 1990
Tomorrow we fly to Tucson in Arizona and then on to the Napa Valley. I have just been out this evening, nipping out secondary buds and tendrils—a most seductive sensation. You hold the thrusting main stem gently but firmly and nip out the fresh, unnecessary growth with a sharp

thumbnail. The vines are, in their different stages, very healthy and I am to leave them for three weeks clean and clear of all but their naked little selves. We've had no rain for nearly a month, but they seem to love it. Rain is forecast for tomorrow, but by then we will be in the air.

When we returned from America just three weeks later the vineyard looked like an explosion in a garden centre. Pruning was a therapeutic orgy and the leaf colours were spectacular. As autumn approached the effect was a glorious vegetative aurora borealis.

In February 1991, I cut the single canes I had encouraged all through the last summer back to the height of the first wire, and removed any extraneous spurs from lower down. Throughout the winter I had dug in wood ash as it became available to help temper the acidic soils in the garden. Vines prefer a more alkaline soil. I treated the vineyard to a generous dose of fishbone and bulls' blood fertilizer and left the rest to the weather.

Due to a late frost in May, budding was set back some weeks and for a while I thought I had lost everything. So did the the vine growers of Bordeaux, where I was at the time. They didn't give a damn about my vineyard! The buds did develop, however, and growth accelerated with Wagnerian vigour as I sung The Ride of the Valkyries daily between the rows.

I treated them all like pedigree racehorses and by early autumn I had vines as spectacular as Desert Orchid. At the time of writing, I wait to prune the bare new canes of late winter 1991, leaving enough new wood to throw out six new spurs on each, the vines supported on the trellis wires like rows of Ys. Next year I should be able to harvest a modest vintage—but don't quote me on that.

Ralph's Vineyard Diary—Stop Press
February 21st 1992
I have acquired some Pinot Noir and Chardonnay from David Shaw of Nutbourne Manor Winery (a good luck gift) to plant in April in what I have discovered to be a 'hotspot' in the garden.

April 1st 1992
Decided to take out of hibernation the Pinot Noir and Chardonnay vines. I asked St Derek if he would dig a shallow trench to lay them out while we decided how to mark out the new vines and dig the holes. He did it in the rain which was good for the vines but not good for Derek, even though he's a saint. We counted 70 vines when the job was done, which is a very generous gift.

April 2nd 1992
St Derek marked out new rows in the 'hotspot' of the garden, close to the wall in the north east corner. The vines closest to that corner indicate much more vigour in their growth. St Derek dug 60 holes today, an amazing feat, and without my help too. I noticed when he had finished that the mud on his boots made him look six inches taller—a fine figure of a man.

April 3rd 1992
It rained heavily and the vines were planted between downpours. A giant step for the vines but a wet neck for St Derek. We kept five of each variety back in pots in case any of the planted ones don't strike and bud. One thing you don't want in a vineyard is an irregular gap. It is unaesthetic.

April 8th 1992
The day before our general election. The atmosphere is rife with speculation. It seems to be a particularly significant contest for the hearts and

minds of Britain and, rather too emphatically, their pockets. Everyone seems to be voting for themselves, which is selfish, of course. Only voting for others is real democracy. I smell disaster. In thirteen years we have forgotten our compassion. The weather is getting warmer. It makes people complacent, but my established vines resolutely refuse to bud. Probably waiting to see who wins the election.

April 9th 1992
Election day. A real spring day. There is hope in the air. Maybe a change of government is imminent. But why don't my vines show signs of life? Maybe vines can prophesy.

By midnight it was becoming clear. We stay up to watch the inevitable. My vines were right. They knew the outcome already. No bogus spring day of a new dawn was going to entice them out of hibernation.

April 10th 1992
In despair I draw a headless chicken and write the caption, '—and now we can put it all behind us and forge ahead.' At 7.20 a.m. I fax it to the *Guardian* for their Saturday edition. My vines will have to suffer 5 more years of Tory rule. But at least they have got a home, and they get welfare. No one can privatise them while I'm around and they get free health checks. They are fully employed. I read the Citizen's Charter to them but they still refuse to bud in spite of the warmth. They know something we don't know.

April 12th 1992
I have named a vine after Neil Kinnock in honour of his brave fight for office. Saint Neil. He has a place in the warmest area in the vineyard, on the left, next to Saint Glenys.

CALIFORNIA

Heading straight for Tucson Arizona when we have just been invited by Sterling Vineyards to visit the Napa valley winegrowing region may seem, to even the most perceptive wine buff, a little perverse. Tucson is known mainly for its cactus juice and wild west spittoons. Its local drink, hooch, brewed in covered wagons from the jealously preserved gargle of parched pioneers suffering from chronic dehydration, is so rough that swallowing a prickly pear would be a velvet experience by comparison. We must have known something before making the serious decision to pay a visit.

In a small place called Oracle, outside Tucson, a massive and awe-inspiring venture is underway. Eight people have been incarcerated inside a monumental glass Aztec temple called Biosphere 2, along with 3,800 species of animal, fish, fowl and insect for a period of two years, sealed off from the outside world (Biosphere 1). Their environment consists of a rainforest, a savanna, a desert, an ocean with wave patterns and filtering complex in an underground vault, a stream, marshes, a rice paddy, vegetable gardens and a vineyard. Yes, a vineyard. We expected to see it and we went there with that justifying objective in

BUZZARD'S EYE-VIEW of the NAPA Valley

Ralph STEADman

mind. However, the vines were still at the root-stock stage and were not produced as evidence of progress.

Less than three months after internment the Biosphere is now troubled. The eight internees are suffocating. At the time of writing there has been some sickness—but no one yet has gone weird, at least no weirder than they are already. That in itself has to be stranger than you or me.

We were shown around by Johnny Allen, alias Dolphin, creator, dreamer, and Father of Biosphere 2. We met Tango, a publishing beauty of Synergetic Books; Flash, Johnny's wife and co-dreamer; Sahara, an Amazon lady who tends the animals; and Harlequin who will be serving the vineyard's every need. This is a 1960s hippy dream come true, backed by Texas billionaire Edward Bass, a dreamer himself, who hopes to test space environments for long stays outside the earth's atmosphere, and maybe discover new life-sustaining patterns for us here on earth.

Harlequin, the gardener and vigneron, was keen to spoil the vines with a kindness best suited to tomatoes, and her consummate attention may

well produce an overlush grape not particularly suitable for winemaking. Drainage will be a big problem. If the vine does not have to fight for survival or have the facility to dig deep for sustenance it will have a shallow taste. The base of this vast edifice is cut off from the earth's crust by sheet stainless steel, set in concrete. No vine can penetrate that. The odds are formidable. Even if you cut yourself off from Biosphere 1, you still need the core of our world. You need to be plugged

BIOSPHERE 2. ORACLE TUSCON. ARIZONA
Ralph STEADman 90.

in. Apart from the sun, the core is where the rest of the energy must come from to sustain life. Even in Biosphere 2, no man is an island. But people are trying, people are trying, and trying is the stuff of it.

We took the train from Tucson. The desert stretched for miles and hundreds of miles, re-affirming a latent fear that one day that is what God intends, if God intends anything at all. He

Between Tucson and Yuma, Amtrack Journey, Dawn

may really only be thinking of Pluto or Uranus, or stars beyond our galaxy which have no vineyards at all, or may be they do. Not only vineyards but wineyards. Grapes which don't even need fermenting. They simply grow on the bough and when you pick them you squeeze the juice straight into a glass and drink it as you would any decent Bordeaux or Chardonnay.

That is the dream of California. It is a land full of promise where dreamers dream of wines which grow themselves, ferment themselves and offer themselves up as a nectar ready for exquisite consumption. Why not? Everything else happens in America. If they are going to make wine, it may as well be instant. Fast wines for the now sensation. Eventually wine will pour from taps into kitchen sinks and water will be a thing of the past. A Cabernet Sauvignon will be the same in 2090 as it will be in 2000. Nothing will be different. The winegrowing techniques of the Napa valley are developing so fast that variables in climate, rainfall, sunshine, harvesting and fermentation will soon be mastered to the degree that they are exactly the same from year to year. The wine is delicious and, of course, is getting even better. I doubt, however, it will touch the idiosyncratic diversity common to the regions and micro-climates of Europe, even though California has emulated all the great techniques and art that European wines can offer.

American wines are slowly but surely reaching their peak, and their variety will gently but effectively level out to yield a kind of constant perfection. I was amazed by the quanlity (yes, quanlity) of Californian wines but I felt that the desire to achieve a specific balance of excellence cancelled out any further developments, other than that of mass-produced quality. No bad thing

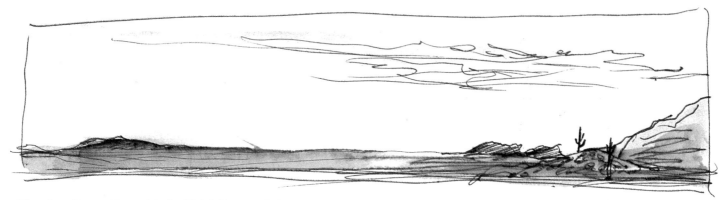

View from Room, Conquistador Hotel, Tucson, Arizona

in itself. But if you efface the differences which make the tasting of wine an unexpected delight, a disappointment even, sometimes a lottery, and always a personal discovery, then you deny the essential joys of wine tasting. Without that variable factor, wine is just another drink. Enjoy American wine while it excels itself from year to year. Enjoy it before it reaches perfection and a price beyond its precocious achievement.

Desert Wind Power

Paul Kenney, Vineyard Manager, Sterling Vineyards

Up on Diamond Mountain we have no frost protection. All the cold air drains from the hillside, so it's warm up there. What the wind machines do is to mix the hot air with the cold air below. That'll give you five degrees more protection. But sprinklers give you a good eight degrees protection, so water is your protection choice if it is available.

The frost, I hate that time of year. That's the worst. By 9 o'clock at night you've got to be by the phone and it goes on like that through March, April and May. Three months stuck by the phone at night and you never know when it's going to go off.
Ralph: *And I thought it was all romance.*

Your palate changes in this business. As a kid you could go out and buy a three-dollar bottle without a cork in it and live high up on the hog, but you get real spoiled.

Paul Kenney: *We have a vineyard here called The Three Palms. Where the creek overflows it just pushes over all the granite and sandstone. When they planted* *that vineyard they dug out the rock and added a little bit of soil. The vines had to work their way down and find a little bit of water but they made great wine.*

Section through LARGEST VINEYARD *in the* WORLD. SAN BERNABE. *(Repeat four times for* FULL PANORAMIC EFFECT*)*

Sterling Three Palms 1986 It was time to try something rather special among all the common good. I searched my modest collection of '86s in the cellar and decided to go NAPA. The bottle beckoned to me like a neglected dog. I took it by the neck and bore it aloft to the kitchen like an expert dog-handler teaching a hound of hell a few tricks. The cork eased out of the bottle like the well-oiled piston of a giant Canadian Pacific Railway train. A whiff of the cork was enough to tell me that this was no ordinary old tipple and I was tempted to replace the cork and go out to the off licence for a Vin de Pays. That's the problem with fine wines. They are so irresistible and yet so collectable also. I advise you, if possible, always to buy two of something you intend to lay down. Otherwise you feel tormented, denuding your collection before its time. This would have been a gorgeous wine to see the next century in with. However, it has gone, but it is not forgotten and the winemaker who created it, Bill Dyer, is a modest man, as are so many real masters. He is not forgotten, either, and I toasted him in the rich dewy strength of his own creation. He has managed to temper the oakiness with a blend of grapes which are holding their own against the muscle of wood.

Claudia Conlon, Public Relations, Sterling Winery

Peter Newton launched an international paper brokerage in San Francisco which sold toilet paper. With British pounds in mind he called it Sterling International. In 1964 he declared, 'I'm going to build me the most fancy thing—a vineyard.' He and his henchmen were all wine lovers. They bought 50 acres right near Calistoga. They planted everything they could without knowing anything about microclimates. In those days you didn't need to spend 40,000 dollars an acre—you'd make friends with the farmer and shake hands on the deal. They did just that.

I have to love this place for deeper reasons than wine interests because it was an Indian burial ground.

Here's our winery. It was built by an Englishman named Martin Waterfield. Quite a renaissance man and a bit of a nut, came back from Mykonos with a design for a winery—he didn't like tourists so he left the bathrooms out.

So visualise the way it used to be: waving fields of wild oats—this is the German valley—the Berringers, the Krugs, very orderly, anal-retentive. Over in the Sonoma Valley on the other side it's the Italians, fun-loving, freer. This land, we say, is the best because it is the stressiest.

MOTEL

SMUCK
FINE
WINE

FREE
TV
POOL
WINE
TASTING
BURGERS

BUCK
WAYNE
Antiques
om. lab

PINNA

NO
PARKING

EL CABANOS
Mexican
Food

TV
LOUNGE

JERK
CHICKEN
ORDERS

TAXI

HOT
DOG

Wine Trail Route 29 to Calistoga - NAPA

now LEASING CONTACT 706 0456
WINE TRAIN
NORTH
INTERSTATE CALIFORNIA 29
One HELLUVA GRAPE IN
ZIP CLEANERS
Paint SHOP
SOUND SERVICES CENTER Inc.
CLINT GULCH WINERY
BUCKWEET WINES
Custom Valet CLEANER
YARD SALE
Ralph STEADman 90

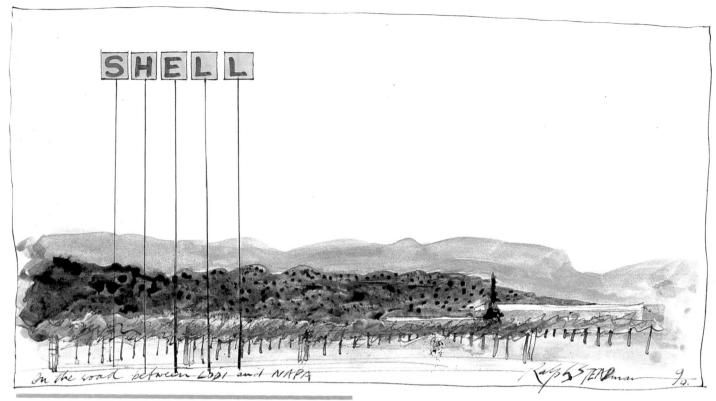

On the road between Lodi and NAPA   Ralph STEADman 90.

Claudia Conlon: *Napa is like a 26-mile-long small town. The county town is Napa. We call it Napa and the Napkins live there. Napkins are very sleepy and the town is very sleepy. Pretty much the original workforce. I think originally they were Chinese sailors from Maire Island who helped René de Rosa plant the vines at Winery Lake. There were no Mexicans then.*

Napa is a vaguely banana-shaped valley situated immediately north of San Francisco Bay. The Bay sends its thick fogs up through the valley in the early morning on cold air currents. The further north you travel up the valley, the warmer it gets. In summer it is not unusual to find an 11°C (20°F) difference between north and south. Winegrowers, like Guy Devaux, a French (yes, French)

Reflection on Phylloxera in California

There is well-founded speculation circulating that the pressure on agriculture to limit the number of varieties of any particular vegetable or fruit to a few streamlined examples, for ease of marketing, is having a disastrous effect on the wellbeing of nature's balance of complexity. Concentration on single varieties renders them vulnerable to disease. An Andean farmer working on a subsistence-farming plot can have as many as 60 different varieties of potato growing at the same time which reduces the danger of pest attack to virtually nil. A single variety is vulnerable to total annihilation. The apple industry in France has reduced its 300 varieties of apple to just three for maximum yield which one scourge of capsid bugs, sawfly, rust, scab, water core, canker, honey fungus, woolly aphids, bitter pit and apple slime could desecrate in a single festival of disease. An

increase in chemical treatment would do the rest. I mention this only because there is news that 60,000 acres of vines in the Napa Valley, previously resistant to phylloxera, are now suffering from the fatal effects of this infamous bug. Could this, I wonder, have something to do with the intensive specialisation in grape varieties, a current trend in that region? Chardonnay, Cabernet Sauvignon, Sauvignon Blanc and, to a lesser extent, Zinfandel are the buzz varieties in the market place at the moment, practically to the exclusion of everything else. Inbreeding and rarification weakens all organic life. The aristocracy can tell you that. Maybe winegrowers are in danger of propagating a whole generation of chinless wonders in the same way. Variety may not suit the souless marketplace but it is still the spice of life.

vigneron and President of sparkling-wine producer Domaine Mumm, uses the eastern slopes, western slopes and the valley floor in his quest to identify the most interesting microclimates and conditions for maximum complexity in his grapes. Guy Devaux also buys grapes from independent grape growers in his search for answers to questions that intrigue him. At the moment he uses mainly Pinot Noir and Chardonnay grapes for his Cuvée Napa, known as Brut Prestige in America (60% Pinot Noir and 40% Chardonnay). The Pinot Noir adds smoothness to the sharper Chardonnay grape. He believes that, for the true enjoyment of wine, all the senses must be involved. The eyes, particularly, play an important part in adjusting the rest of our senses to accept and appreciate an experience. So the subtlety in colour of his white sparkling wines is most important to him. That pinkish (blush!), yellowish, or even autumnal look to a white wine triggers an aesthetic response augmenting the first taste on the palate—so very French. And Guy Devaux claims that his vinification practices are closer to the *méthode champenoise* than those of anyone else in the valley. Yet he is not a plagiarist, he says; since champagne already exists, there is no point in making a copy. He makes an original sparkling wine.

Since the beginning of the twentieth century the Napa valley has suffered from the effects of the phylloxera bug, the changing fortunes of farmers and, particularly, Prohibition. Most of the valley was grubbed out to make room for other fruits, especially prunes, of course, which became the big mover. The only wine made during Prohibition was sacramental wine and wine 'for medicinal purposes', which was how producers like the Martini family survived. In the 1960s a new interest in wine developed and many of the flower generation moved up the Napa valley from San Francisco looking for work or mind-expanding experiences. They found grape-picking instead and, I suspect, a natural affinity for the product. Many settled and became winegrowers themselves, wealthy or otherwise, gaining knowledge and degrees from the University of California Viticulture Department at Davis, and nerve centre of all accumulated research on the subject of wine. This centre probably accounts for the common

Route 29. NAPA Valley.

philosophy among winegrowers in the region. It also accounts for my feeling that a general sterility of procedure will set in as the individual grower disappears.

Haveaniceday Grand Cru: Wine tasting on Highway 29

Californian wine is big business. Highway 29 runs right up through the valley and serves as the main artery for the hordes of tourists who pour into the region for tastings which have become as popular now as a trip to Disneyland. Then came the Wine Train, a kind of boozer's Orient Express running parallel to the road. The tourist trade has burgeoned and the train now serves as a safer way to taste as many wines as you can get down on the

tour without getting involved in a serious drink-drive bust.

All tasting reception centres are geared to service the multitudes, hungry and thirsty for knowledge and experience of this newest of American pastimes. You clamber aboard at the town of Napa, you drink at the stopovers and you fall off in St Helena, halfway up the valley. If you could go any further you probably wouldn't make it unless you simply suck and spit as a true taster would; a difficult task once you succumb to the holiday mode. And you will, if you are basically a wine slob like me and my friends.

We stayed at Sterling Vineyards in Calistoga, a few miles north of St Helena at the top end of the valley. Calistoga used to be a place where Indians came to cure their arthritis by rolling in the hot mud of natural geysers. A nineteenth-century entrepreneur decided to exploit this phenomenon and invited prospective investors up from San Francisco to take mineral baths and drink wine. The area, he hoped, would become the Saratoga (a famous East Coast spa) of California. Before his introductory speech, though, he got drunk and welcomed his guests to what he slurred would become 'the—hic—Calistoga of Sara-fornia'. Whichever way you say it the name schtuck.

The Sterling winery is a Greek-style palace built on a steep mid-valley knoll and is reached by cable

Kettleman City — Mexican Town — San.

On the road to LEMOORE — a fundamentalist's PARADISE — Ralph STEADman 90

car if you are the public, and private road if you are a guest and don't like heights. The winery looks down majestically over what could be called its kingdom. A set of antique bells, the St Dunstan's Bells, were transported from London and set into a circular headed tower. They peel out every quarter of an hour over vineyards which produce a range of wines of diverse character. Two of Sterling's three main vineyards, Diamond Mountain and Three Palms, are conveniently spread out down below around their palace. The third main vineyard, Winery Lake, is situated further south near the town of Napa. There are fourteen vineyards in all, covering well over 400 ha (1,000 acres). This is only a fraction of the planted area of the Napa valley itself, which has in excess of 12,140 ha (30,000 acres). Yet this is still only seven per cent of California's total vineyard acreage, yielding a mere four per cent of California's total wine production.

Diamond Mountain is fierce and rugged terrain. Hard work and ingenuity coax a complex range of Chardonnay, Cabernet Sauvignon, Merlot and Cabernet Franc from a tough soil in rattlesnake country. Robert Louis Stevenson spent his honeymoon in the region with his new wife Fanny, and Calistogans declare with pride that he wrote 'And the wine is bottled poetry' about their very wines. I think he actually said 'And their wines are bottled properly'. They also claim that he wrote some of *Treasure Island* in Calistoga, even though, according to his stepson Lloyd Osborne, he wrote it chapter by chapter from his sickbed in Scotland inspired by a map of an imaginary island drawn by Lloyd Osborne himself.

When the Sterling vineyards were in Coca-Cola's ownership, the company had a problem controlling land erosion on the steep terraced slopes of Diamond Mountain. They paid heavily for consultancy engineers to figure out a way to

in Valley — Ralph STEADman 90

THE MONTEREY WINERY WITH THE THIEVING INDIGENOUS GRAPE SEAGULLS.
Ralph STEADman Gonzales Ca%

control it. Cement was their solution, acres of it, which seemed, even to Coca-Cola, like a crude idea in such an area of natural beauty. A Spaniard called Rodrigo Delego lived on Diamond Mountain with his three-legged dog called Lobo. He was a farmer and knew the ways of the land. He suggested the use of gusanos, which means 'worm' in Spanish. These are great thick rubber hoses, in sections, which can be used to direct the rainwater like drainpipes down the slopes into culverts at the base of the mountain. During the summer months, the sections can be turned sideways at each terrace to allow access for tractors and other farm machinery. It solved the prob-

lem and saved Coca-Cola millions, and is still in use. Rodrigo got no promotion, no bonus, no nothing, not even recognition. They didn't even get him another three-legged dog when Lobo died. He lives on Diamond Mountain on his own.

On Diamond Mountain there is a ghost winery, built in 1888, in three tiers of stone, brick and wood on a sharp rise which made good use of gravity to process the grapes which were received at the top entrance. They were crushed on the top floor. They were fermented on the floor below, then gravity-fed to be racked off for cask ageing below that, then racked down yet again for bottling and cellaring in caves which go right back

First Hint on Route 5

The American Way—high-density simplification—a vine-growing technique spreading like must from a bucket through the wine industry. Canopy protection is provided by Mexican workers who will stand around all day for next to nothing protecting the grapes from the sun's midday intensity.

The S-Method—a stress-provoking configuration. The spurs are forced to grow downwards on the left-hand cordon causing a confusion which adds complexity to the grape. On the same plant the upward right-hand cordon is allowed rampant free rein which further confuses the main vine stem. The two grape harvests are mixed.

The Eiffel Double Vine Graft. Intensifies the sugar and tannin thrust upwards from the root system to a single crop of grapes. It reminds an American grower of France and helps him to imagine that his efforts are achieving a continental bouquet in the finished product.

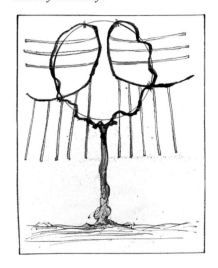

The Double Spiral Curtain. Idiosyncratic style producing a weirdness in the grape flavour more suited to freak varietals like Cabernet-Grenache and Folle-Blanche-Gewürzentraminer-Alphonse-Lavallée.

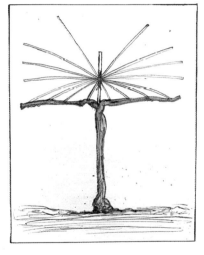

The 'Star Burst Convergence' concentrates the vine's attention and develops a grape rich in tannin and very sweet, suited to a dessert wine with a bouquet that simply explodes in your pants.

The 'Scaffold' method suits the intensive commercialisation of the wine industry, combining a simple growing technique with an American's love of flaunting his achievements.

Cactic Loxera: caused by the heat a vine thrives on—but far too much of it. A vine gets comfortable, has a kind protector and lives for today. Its roots grow upwards and it feeds off itself. The roots become the fruit and offer a grape of woody, fibrous and sandy texture. The pioneers made covered wagon hooch from such stricken plants in old spitoons and forged a taste for wines which maybe explains a preference for intense oak maturation common in most NAPA valley wines today. Along with SCUPPERNONG (Vitis rotundifolia), Riverbank grape (Vitis riparia), Vitis labrusca and Vitis aestivalis, the Summer grape, Cactic Loxera-infected vines are the only truly indigenous grape varieties in North America, appreciated for their snake-bite aftertaste.

Pricklitic Pearvitalis or heat rash affects all desert-grown grapes eventually. A grape from a vine in this condition will produce a wine of such harsh and piercing acidity that if drunk to excess, I was reliably informed, 'yer ass'll drop off!'

Americanus Identivoid Problematico. A strange square fungal area appears on the vine wood just prior to 'vendange' time in late September indicating a strange complexity in the vine's sense of well-being brought on by some insecurity regarding the vine's pedigree and its status as a vintage crop of world class.

Noble Rot—the aristocratic mould—BOTRYTIS Cinerea—Pourriture NOBLE. A technique of making wines from BOTRYTIS-infected vines which NAPA valley winegrowers are desperate to encourage in their royalty-hungry climate.

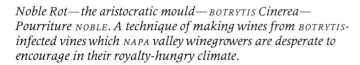

Prohibitinisticus Erectus. A peculiarly American viticulture complaint—deep within the psyche of every winegrower in America lies the dormant fear of a new surge of puritanism which last emerged in the 20's and caused acres of fine growing vines to be grubbed out in favour of prunes and other worthy products. If a winegrower allows those puritan feelings full rein a sensitive vine suffers guilt tremors and loses its vigour in favour of an austere growth pattern more suited to the 'new decency' currently popular—such vines stiffen and do not need a stake support system.

Vitis Paranoica Phylloxterror Vastatrix. Bad vibes travel fast and the slightest talk in a vineyard of the dreaded aphid phylloxera is considered bad luck, though groundless in America until recently since pure American vine rootstocks are resistant to the disease. Here we see a case of just plain old paranoia—a national pastime often transmitted to an impressionable vine by a screwed-up wine grower.

into the hillside. Wine was collected for transportation from the front double-doored entrance let into a large, cool, stone construction, which was also sturdy enough to support the incline of buildings above it.

An air of quiet mystery hung about the place in the shaded heat of the day. If you stand motionless and let the heavy, somnolent atmosphere seep into your senses, you can almost hear the fermenting must bubbling like a shallow mountain stream over rounded pebbles. Ghost Winery, brooding and lonely, hunkers like a resentful old giant into its mountain resting place, a decaying monument to cottage-industry winemaking long gone—the antithesis of today's brittle science technology and hard-nosed marketing.

It was our last stop before making our way south again, skirting around San Francisco down into the San Joaquin valley, the salad bowl of America. The region is vast, flat and sprawls like a desolate planet. We passed what is claimed to be the biggest vineyard in the world, the 3,400 ha (8,500 acre) San Bernabe vineyard, south of King City. If you stand at its edge, you cannot see its ends in either direction. They are the horizon of the landscape. The harvest must be transported in refrigerated trucks to wineries 30 miles (48 km) away to prevent premature fermentation.

The vineyards of Monterey are practically the same, stretching out across a flat featureless blank from Tula, 4 miles (6.4 km) north of Gonzales (where the Monterey vineyards winery is) to San Lucas 45 miles (72 km) to the south, offering a wide growing range to suit a variety of grapes.

Highway 101 spans the vineyards and the endless green vegetable acres like packing tape around a vast parcel. The little Mexican worker's town of Gonzales is just an afterthought of cheap bunker-like buildings on either side of the road. It didn't appear to have ever seen better days, nor was it ever likely to. It was more like a packing station than a town, with the busy highway running right through its heart.

The early morning mists which roll in from the Pacific suffocate the whole region until the sun of late morning burns them off and reveals nothing but the endless expanse which you knew instinctively was there anyway. Monterey, nevertheless, is situated on the flat floor of a vast valley bordered on the east side by the Diablo Mountains and on the west by the Santa Lucia range, which runs down the coast from Monterey to San Simeon (home of the Hearst newspaper family). This creates a kind of tunnel which channels the constantly moving cold marine air in with the thermal currents up and down the valley.

Monterey's grapes flourish in this combination of cool, damp, sea mists from Monterey Bay and the hot midday temperatures of the endless flatlands. The vines in Monterey start budding in late February. Chardonnay is in bloom by late April. The fruit is harvested in the first week in October, giving the grapes a lengthy 150 days on the vine, compared with the 100 days that is usual in France. Such a long, slow growing season accounts for the powerful flavours and concentration of fruit. At the same time, steady and even weather guarantees ample harvests.

Phil Franscioni, one of the winemakers for Monterey Vineyards, conducts many experiments with different kinds of French and American oak barrels to lend different complexities to the heart and flavour of his wines. There are not many variables in the weather every year, and no distinct microclimates. The region is rigidly uniform, so cellar experiments proliferate, almost as a compensating factor. Recently the winery has been fire-forming Limousin oak staves which burns the natural sugars and starches in the wood and carmelizes them. This has the effect of thickening the flavour of the wines and imparting a toasty aroma.

I was shown a quite brilliant piece of lateral thinking in the Monterey Vineyards cellar. The problem is how to maximise a wine's extraction of wood flavour while it is in cask. The Monterey

The HABITUES of exclusive tastings, these creatures roam from WINERY to WINERY under the guise of an aficionado, and gulp the stuff straight down from the PIPETTE used to draw off a sample for those who would otherwise sip and suck delicately to appreciate the complexities of fine WINES.

NOT SO THE SLOB. He waits until the tasting party has moved on to experience further viticultural delights of the PALATE while he helps himself . . . His motto: If I'm gonna taste it—I need a lot of it!

solution is to instruct the coopers to build inside each barrel a radiating series of oak fins, rather like the spokes of a wheel. The surface area of wood is therefore increased tenfold without decreasing the volume of the barrel significantly. This technique imparts to the wine a much oakier flavour than usual. Whether that can be considered a bonus in the appreciation of wine is a matter of opinion, but the strongly flavoured grapes from this region seem to stand up magnificently to the test. The wines we tasted, the 1988 and 1989 Chardonnays and Cabernet Sauvignons, were as good as anything we had tried 'up the Napa'.

Phil Franscioni is so committed to his chosen profession that he even got married in front of an altar made of wine barrels in the winery, where a priest agreed to perform the ceremony. The reception was held in the barrel room and the wedding cake was cut in the sunshine glow of a spectacular stained-glass window of grapes and vines. He didn't tell me where they spent their honeymoon, but rumour has it that it was in an empty vat.

Though once owned by Coca-Cola, Monterey Vineyards has survived, and seems to flourish unscathed. As far as I know there isn't a bug resilient enough to attack and wipe out Cocanis Colaniteptaranus, the parasitic creeper that bears the fizzy sweet berries from which Coke is made. Those bugs that have tried to floor the creeper end up with rotten teeth. On occasion, the gassy juice ferments in the stomach, effervesces furiously,

Phil Franscioni, Winemaker, Monterey Winery

In France the grapes have 100 days on the vine from bloom to harvest. We harvest at the same time—but we are in bloom in May, when theirs are just starting to push. That's where we get our flavours and concentration of fruit.

These barrels have just been shaved. Now they've got CO_2 in—so don't stick your nose in there!

Ralph: *Say it again, Hal, what do you really think of it?*
Hal: *It's ripe, it's quite ripe. Hell of a good wine. A hell of a goddam good wine.*

Tucker Catlin, Winemaker, ex. Sterling Vineyards

I don't think Americans understand wine in the pleasure sense. It's like a ball game. That's the fixation in America: who won the contest? I think the French couldn't care less who won a tasting. Everybody has a different personality. That's what's fun about people and that's what's fun about wine. America doesn't understand that. America thinks someone should win, someone should lose. It's not the freedom to enjoy. Americans say there's one personality I like and I don't like anything else.

Light through a stained-glass window pours over vats of CHARDONNAY 1989 *at the* MONTEREY *Winery, Gonzales, California*

GUY DEVAUX – High Priest of Sparkling WINE   Ralph STEADman

and the insect explodes. Pity. If there had been a phylloxera-type bug that thrived on such a trip, the world may have been a better place to live in.

GOPHER DAMAGE—
A kind of 3-cornered RODENT FEEDING FRENZY ABOVE the ROOT OF A VINE.

MONTEREY WINERY— GONZALES. California.

Ralph STEADman

Guy Devaux, President, Domaine Mumm

All our operations are pretty well automated. That permits us to use untrained labour—Mexican. The only thing they do is to start or stop the press. All the other techniques are done automatically by the computer.

[On the Méthode Champenoise.] What is fermentation? The grape juice is composed roughly of water, sugar and acid, and in the skin of the grapes you find yeasts which, in contact with the juice and the sugar, are going to be the agents of the fermentation. They are going to feed on the sugar and, as a by-product of their activity, they are going to produce alcohol and carbon dioxide. During the first fermentation the carbon dioxide is a dangerous thing we try to get rid of. Pipes on top of the tanks take the carbon dioxide out fast. At the end of the fermentation the sugar has been consumed, it's no longer juice but wine. A second fermentation takes place in the bottle. The carbon dioxide can no longer escape and it dissolves itself into the wine. When you remove the seal, carbon dioxide wants to get out. This is what makes the fizz in sparkling wine.

Greg Fowler, Winemaker, Domaine Mumm

In real heat the vines will pull carbohydrates back out of the grape. The vine goes into a survival mode, doesn't care about reproducing. You can watch the berries shrivel. It happened in '81.

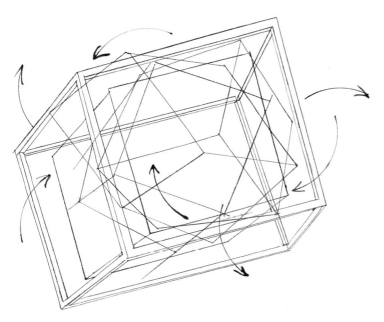

The Computerized Méthode Champenoise Giro Pallet. How best can I describe it to you? A steel cubic frame contains another steel cubic frame which is supported by mobile sprockets on ratchet drive gears allowing mobility through 360 degrees— in all directions! The end result is rather like a MULTI-STOREY *milk crate. How they worked that one out god only knows but it beats hourly turning of a million bottles by hand until the bottles of bubbly are all upside down with the sediment settled in the neck of the bottle ready for extraction. The neck is then* FROZEN *which traps the sediment. This 'ice cork' is then blown out by the gas in the wine and replaced by a proper cork—and* BINGO! *Crystal clear sparkling wine. Got it?*

NAPA Valley WINE TOUR TASTING w

I'm a NAPA Valley Wine Snob.

WINE TRAIN

Ralph STEADman 9o

PERU

While on a visit to Peru in June 1991 at the invitation of the Pachamama (Mother Earth) Society, we flew by helicopter from coastal Paracas inland over desert to view the strange Nasca lines, a mysterious configuration of geometric shapes and symbolic figures drawn into the surface of a flat plateau. On the way back we flew over a story-book oasis and several vast green areas which stood out of the sandy expanse of desert like huge snooker tables. I was led to believe that they were Peruvian vineyards, but from our flying altitude they looked rather light

Peruvian Desert Vineyard.

and more like asparagus beds. However, they may well have been vineyards and without actually landing to find out I accept the possibility graciously and thus include my rendition of the strange sight. One thing is certain: if they were vines they would not have needed a north-facing slope to gather the sun's power. The rows of tall poplars standing at the southern end of each area provided little or no shade and were probably only a hedge against desert winds. They may well have been provided to give vineyard workers somewhere to shelter in the heat of high noon.

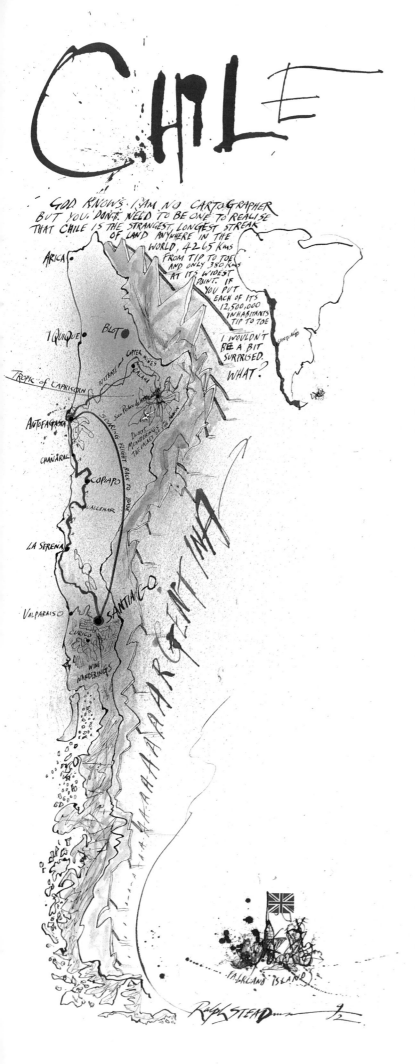

GOD KNOWS, I AM NO CARTOGRAPHER
BUT YOU DON'T NEED TO BE ONE TO REALISE
THAT CHILE IS THE STRANGEST, LONGEST STREAK
OF LAND ANYWHERE IN THE
WORLD, 4265 Kms
FROM TIP TO TOE
AND ONLY 380 Kms
AT ITS WIDEST
POINT. IF
YOU PUT
EACH OF ITS
12,500,000
INHABITANTS
TIP TO TOE
I WOULDN'T
BE A BIT
SURPRISED.
WHAT?

ARICA

IQUIQUE   BLOT

TROPIC OF CAPRICORN

ANTOFAGASTA

CHAÑARAL

COPIAPO

VALLENAR

LA SERENA

VALPARAISO   SANTIAGO

CURICO

WINE
WANDERINGS

ARGENTINA

FALKLAND ISLAND

RalphSTEADman

In Search of O'Higgins

The vines of Chile are the descendants of Bordeaux cuttings brought over in the 1840s by wealthy Chilean mine owners fired with visions of elegant pursuits back home—in the euphoric wake of their Grand Tours of Europe. As though by divine intervention, these cuttings missed the scourge of phylloxera by a matter of a few years: the bug has never crossed the Andes, or the Pacific Ocean, or even the deserts of Atacama to the north, which effectively cuts Chile off from the rest of the world. To the south there is only Antarctica. All this proves that the phylloxera pest doesn't like heights, gets seasick very easily, needs water to survive like the rest of us, and can't fly in winter woollies.

The vines of Chile are whole and ungrafted. They were established by sinking long canes of vine cuttings up to half their length into the rich soils of the temperate central valleys of Maipo, Curicó and Aconcagua around the capital city of Santiago.

The cool Humboldt current caresses Chile's coast all the way down to the tip of its Latin American toes at Cape Horn, which is why the Latins love to dance.

An influx of Catholic priests who accompanied the conquistadors in the 1540s created a demand for sacramental wine to bless the Spanish rampage in its search for gold. It was only Pedro de Valdivia who realised that the real gold of Chile was the soil of the central and southern valleys. He fell in love with the country and founded Santiago in 1541, with his faithful mistress Ines de Suarez, who had fought alongside him. Ironically, it is said, he died near another town he founded called Concepción, at the hands of Mapuche Indians—by being forced to swallow molten gold.

The first vines, the black Pais or 'native' grape, may have arrived from the Canary Islands. There was, however, a black Moscatel variety growing in the foothills of the Andes already and this may have been used to make the first wines.

One hundred years after Valdivia, Vice Admiral John Byron, known as 'Foul Weather Jack', and grandfather of Lord Byron, made his way up through Chile to Santiago with the few surviving sailors from one of his disastrous voyages. He describes wine as rich as Madeira and as cheap as it was plentiful. Its growth and manufacture was so simple: the fertile land and climate ensured unavoidable success.

Early in the nineteenth century the colonial authorities in Spain began to resent this success, and they ordered the destruction of vines in the Northern Provinces, the most prolific region. Merchants from Cádiz were complaining that the Spanish wine industry was suffering because it was they who were supposed to supply the colonies.

In 1810 a coup d'état of patriot forces deposed the Spanish authorities, and set up a junta in Santiago. Civil war erupted and patriot forces led by a Chilean of Irish descent called Bernardo O'Higgins and John MacKenna, a professional soldier and fellow Irishman, fought to free Chile from Spanish rule. The patriots suffered a terrible defeat at Rancagua in 1814 and O'Higgins fled with 120 men to Buenos Aires, hiding on the way in some magnificent old cellars built of mud bricks, lime and white of egg. These cellars are claimed to be the very ones which are used today by Viña Santa Rita to store their 120 Cabernet Sauvignon, 120 Sauvignon Blanc and 120 Merlot, named or rather numbered in honour of these brave sons of Chile. There is doubt surrounding this claim and it is more likely that the men hid 120 yards down the road in some less conspicuous hole in the ground, but the 'Legend of the 120' holds good in the interests of tourism and commerce.

In 1817, Bernardo O'Higgins returned to Chile across the Cordillera de los Andes, joined by an Argentinian leader, José de San Martín, with an army now 3,600 men strong, growing as it travelled, 'the army of the Andes'. O'Higgins was a Hannibal without elephants, and his men were a fearsome bunch, hooting and whooping like demented peacocks on market day. They beat the royalist troops at Chacabuco and entered Santiago in triumph with Chileans well and truly on their side. Bernardo was the son of Ambrosio O'Higgins, an officer of the Spanish Crown in Peru. Nobody imagined that these men were desperate and the Spaniards forgot that Chile was under siege, not from outsiders—the Spaniards themselves had already arrived and taken over. These men were from within. They were fighting for rights and self-government. They fought with righteous zeal. Such men always do. Nothing has changed.

At that time the Spanish government ruled like selfish gods as did all other colonial powers. They forbade the owning of ships by South Americans—or consignments of goods capable of making a profit. Only Spaniards could live in South America alongside the indigenous population. No ship from foreign lands could even dock in a South American port. In fact, unless you were Spanish you weren't even human and you never had a mother and the only mother anyway was the Holy Mother of God.

Britain kept out of it and let the wayward Napoleonic soldiers of fortune move in as they inevitably did to take their chances with the oppressed whose land this was. Britain was merely anticipating a new republic with which to trade without lifting a finger. There was a growing demand for copper, nitrates and silver to serve a bright industrial future, and Chile was rich in them all.

So the Spanish were defeated in the central regions of Chile. O'Higgins was made president. He immediately called up an old croney, Lord Thomas Cochrane.

Cochrane didn't need much persuasion since he was not considered an honourable man with the Admiralty. He was, however, a galvaniser of men and turned helpless peasants and geriatric old soldiers into a lean, sleek fighting machine. He drove them north to Peru and Cusco, the seat of Spanish power. He overwhelmed the Spanish and liberated Peru and Chile by sheer magnetic charisma. He was Chile's game-show host of the 1820s.

Together the three leaders liberated a monumental part of South America. They are honoured in street names, Chilean fast foods, and banks. As a matter of fact, their very names were odious to many while they were still alive but regained their popularity after death.

General MacKenna's descendants number two famous Chilean families, the Undurragas of Santa Ana in the Maipo Valley and the Eyzaguirres of Los Vascos. Both families make wine.

With the Spanish power gone, trade opened up with the rest of the world in the 1850s and the wine industry developed under European influence. The traditional Pais grape was replaced in some of the large vineyards with Cabernet Sauvignon, Sauvignon Blanc, Semillon, Riesling, Pinot Noir and Merlot. French oenologists were brought in to advise, and the Chilean wine industry proper got under way.

The Chilean climate and the soils are a perfect combination for wine growing. Mildew and botrytis have never been a problem and of course the phylloxera bug is not a perpetual fear as it is in the rest of the world. It is as though Chile was the one place on earth chosen by a God on one of His better days, gathering all His blessings.

Paolo: Notes from a Desert Diarist

In the middle of nowhere a lone soul's heart beats as strong as anyone's. But day after day, week after week, year in, year out, down the centuries a serious diarist can go mad, not only in the pitiless heat, but locked inside the emptiness that surrounds him. It concentrates the mind to fever pitch and can be the cause of much self-scrutiny.

15th May 1536

'Got up; went outside. Went back in. Sat down. Waited. Got up; looked outside again went back in, sat down, picked up my pen. Dipped it in cactus ink and wrote "Nothing happened".'

Suddenly a donkey passes his window. A strange donkey. Not from around these parts. The lone diarist leaps up and goes outside to watch. He goes indoors again and writes:

'A donkey just went by. Looked it up in my book. There's no such animal in these parts. Must have been a llama with a short neck. Funny colour for a llama. My nails could do with a trim. My book says that donkeys come from Egypt, Ethiopia and Somaliland, roaming wild. They have spread through Turkey, Asia Minor and the Balkans and were domesticated all over Europe by the ninth century. Note: stubborn. Will not reach the New World before the nineteenth century. Hmmm.'

It's a pretty interesting day for a desert diarist. A donkey, real or imagined, is life, and describing it can take at least a page. It's when a second donkey goes by on the same day that things can get a bit hectic. The diarist may get over-excited. He'll need a drink. He can hardly hold his pen as he trembles, searching for the words to capture the sense of occasion:

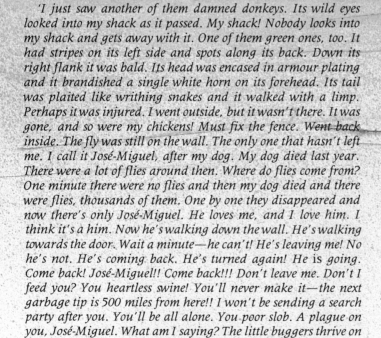

'I just saw another of them damned donkeys. Its wild eyes looked into my shack as it passed. My shack! Nobody looks into my shack and gets away with it. One of them green ones, too. It had stripes on its left side and spots along its back. Down its right flank it was bald. Its head was encased in armour plating and it brandished a single white horn on its forehead. Its tail was plaited like writhing snakes and it walked with a limp. Perhaps it was injured. I went outside, but it wasn't there. It was gone, and so were my chickens! Must fix the fence. Went back inside. The fly was still on the wall. The only one that hasn't left me. I call it José-Miguel, after my dog. My dog died last year. There were a lot of flies around then. Where do flies come from? One minute there were no flies and then my dog died and there were flies, thousands of them. One by one they disappeared and now there's only José-Miguel. He loves me, and I love him. I think it's a him. Now he's walking down the wall. He's walking towards the door. Wait a minute—he can't! He's leaving me! No he's not. He's coming back. He's turned again! He is going. Come back! José-Miguel!! Come back!!! Don't leave me. Don't I feed you? You heartless swine! You'll never make it—the next garbage tip is 500 miles from here!! I won't be sending a search party after you. You'll be all alone. You poor slob. A plague on you, José-Miguel. What am I saying? The little buggers thrive on plagues. OK José-Miguel, I hope you land in a bucket of something pure and wholesome—yes, that's it!—and get sticky wings!'

Nothing else could possibly happen, not today. Not ever, But you can never tell. The desert is forever busy. . . .

1st January 1541

'Woke with a start. Was I dreaming? Heard galloping hooves. Got up. Went to the window. My god! Visitors. Weird strange beasts breathing steam from flared nostrils wearing tin hats. They are followed by a dishevelled mob of what look like foot soldiers, tired and grim and hungry. I walk outside. The leader says he is Pedro, of Valdivia, wherever that is. He has heard tell of gold to the south. If I can tell him where it is he says he'll irrigate my land for free. He says he is a Conquistador and that is what they do, in exchange for gold. When I asked him what colour it was he grabbed one of the tired, the grim and the footsore by the scruff of the neck who pointed a limp finger at my back garden, muttering in a strange tongue. His nails could have done with a trim, I thought. He said "PAIS". I said, "I beg your pardon?" He said "PAIS". It means "native". I fancied he was referring to my vineyard. This year's crop of Pais grapes promises to be the best vintage ever. Then this shining rabble, all metal, spikes and snorting grandeur, rode roughshod through it all, eating the grapes, trampling my shack and drinking all my water, then digging a canal all the way up to the Andes behind my shack before going their way south in peace, whooping and chanting "Freedom to all Chileans!" An emaciated priest blessed my new-found dereliction with the words "Cabernet Sauvignon", which sounded Greek to me. Then he handed me a stick and told me to plant it before stumbling off to keep up with the others.'

26th March 1813

'Got up. Funny day. I finally got around to planting that stick the priest gave me in 1541. Fancied I heard the sound of gunfire. I really must empty the cesspit—and cut my toenails. Passing travellers always point them out. Though it seems the whole of Chile is up in arms people keep talking about my feet. Exhausted travellers fall inside my shack, apologise, mention my feet, and the cesspit, then fall outside again into the midday sun.'

12th March 1814

'Woken in the night by squabbling outside my window. Nobody seems to know what belongs to whom. Nobody wants my shack and every night I praise the Lord. This year's crop from that stick was bumper and is bubbling away like El Tatio geysers steaming at dawn. Must empty the cesspit and spread it around. I think my spring is drying up. Haven't had rain for 200 years. Thank God for the canal. I don't think the Spanish like it here anymore. There's been a flood of them through in the last month. Must stop feeding the vultures. They look a bit bloated.'

12th February 1817

'Got up feeling whacked out. Hell of a commotion in the night. Shouts of "Viva, Bernardo O'Higgins! Rout the Royalist troops! Santiago is Chilean! O'Higgins for president. Freedom for the Chileans—and the Irish!" Went back to bed. The world's going mad.'

PAOLO—the Desert DIARIST.

1st January 1818

'Must fix that hole in my roof. I don't know what caused it but if it rains, I'll catch it in a bucket. Really getting the hang of this grape growing. I took cuttings from that stick. Now got a whole hectare of them. Decided to call the harvest ''Cabernet Sauvignon'' after the priest. He was a topper. God bless his hairy cassock.'

20th August 1820

'Independence! I woke with a start. It had a significant ring to it so I write it down, but I don't know what it means. José-Miguel came back today. It was a good sign and I forgave him for leaving me. He alighted on my nose and I guided him tenderly towards my new pile of garbage.'

10th December 1830

'Woken by a regular hammering on my door. Got up and went to see who was there. Nobody in sight, but on my door was a sign which read, ''The Bernard O'Bins Commemorative Shack.'' It was rather elegant so I left it up. Gold lettering on sun-dried cactus pith.'

3rd September 1839

'Weird wanderers bearing sticks like mine are making their way south. They are polite and elegant. In exchange for water they give me some of their sticks. I give them advice. ''Plant them soon,'' I say. They bless me with words like ''Sauvignon Blanc'' and ''Merlot'', ''Chardonnay'' and ''Pisco Sour'' then move on.'

26th February 1845

'The weird people were right about their sticks. And so was I. I now have a vineyard of rare and fulsome abundance. Foreigners beat on my door and ask for directions and more advice. My fly is ecstatic. He is crazy for the pungent aroma of rotting grape skins.'

5th October 1880

'The place is swarming with passing fortune-seekers and stick bearers. It think it's getting out of hand. Saw a cloud. Hovered about a bit above the shack. Feels like rain. Wonder what it looks like? Never found out. One of them damned desert whirlwinds blew it over the mountains. Anyway, it played havoc with my arthritic big toe.'

4th June 1944

'Things have been a bit quiet lately. People must be busy getting on with things. Not many travellers. Just the odd foreigner carrying works of art. Finding it a problem to store my wine. Give most of it to the odd foreigners.'

3rd August 1956

'Someone just built a street past my shack. Can't get any sleep with all the racket. Strange tin things on four wheels whizz back and forth without stopping to pass the time of day. Think it's time to move on myself. . .'

The diary stops here and nobody knows what happened to this lone voice in the desert. Some say he went into politics and campaigned for public ownership, and some say he just went. Who knows? But his spirit lives on in all those other desolate shacks scattered across the landscape. Other private thoughts, recording everything with an old quill pen dipped in cactus ink:

4th April 1992
'Nothing happened.'

Ralph's Chilean Diary

23rd February 1992

Our first bottle as we reach Santiago is Viña Carmen's 1986 Gran Reserva Cabernet Sauvignon. It was a tannic welcome. The waiter kept the bottle on his table—a most irritating way to drink wine. You wait on his pleasure and not your own. His rhythms were slow and studied as though he was still doing a course on elegant waiting. On the same evening we drink a bottle of Santa Rita Medalla Real Cabernet Sauvignon. This has a more interesting, homespun Chilean taste. It is much sharper and brighter in colour—more the child, and livelier for its innocence.

24th February 1992

The weather is balmy, without humidity, and is very comfortable. People have a gentle disposition and dark hair predominates. I am the only white-haired balding person on the bus we are taking to Valparaiso. The architecture is either modern or jerry-built with a few scattered pieces of colonial elegance, lonely and dust-laden among the cheap signs of old shops and decorations painted directly on to brick walls.

The roads are jammed with blocks of buses trying to negotiate traffic lights which only incense the Latin temperament. Horns blast and orchestrate the tempers of drivers to a crescendo going nowhere. Relax. It's not too hot; relax. Nothing lasts forever. The bus lurches every five minutes and we descend into hell through the seven stages of purgatory. Was it William Burroughs I saw shuffling along in Valparaiso?

25th February 1992

Today the Andes don't exist. We drove two hours on the Pan-American Highway through heavy mist and visibility was about 200 yards. Beyond was just a white background—nothing. The Andes could be a myth, or a huge theatrical cardboard backdrop. We drive through the Maipo Valley at the narrowest point in all of Chile: a mere 90 kilometers (56 miles) across from the Argentine border to the sea.

As we enter Rancagua the sun begins to burn through the mist, but a haze persists. We cross many dry river beds and quite suddenly strike the sunlight and a clearer atmosphere. The mountains rise up beyond the flat valley floor. Huge sweeps of sunflowers and fruit plantations stretch away towards the foothills. Small shrines are dotted along the highway in memory of those who died

Santiago from Cerro San Cristóbal

in road accidents.

The long journey to Curicó was made longer by not knowing how far it was or even who we were going to see. We passed the most English of loca-

hill around which the city is built

Ralph STEADman 9/2

tions, weeping willows with twisted trunks sloping up from the banks of a fast, clean-flowing river. I waved to Christopher Robin, Pooh and Piglet too. It was an idyll and ridiculously English.

We had arrived at the house of Pedro Grand, owner of Nogales, a company which, along with Montes, forms part of a group known as Discover Wine Ltda. This group was established in 1988 by

ERRAZURIZ Panquehue Vineyards, ACONCAGUA Valley

four people with wine in common. They had realised that a big operation was not necessarily the road to success with Chilean wines, and that quality and individual expression might be Chile's leading asset. With every climatic advantage on their side, the four men, Aurelio Montes, Pedro Grand, Alfredo Vidaurre and Douglas Murray, set out to prove that accessibility, understanding, guidance and, above all, a sympathetic love of the essence of wine were elements to be nurtured and passed on to a still sceptical world. A wine tasting was set out for us on a table overlooking a delightful bend in the river. Everything shimmered with dappled light. There were six wines to try.

A 1989 Chardonnay: very meaty. A Sauvignon Blanc, less so, and a 1989 Montes Fumé Blanc, delicate and fresh. Then we moved through three reds: Merlot, very soft; a Cabernet Sauvignon 1991 which was all fruit; and an oak-aged Cabernet Sauvignon, much stronger in flavour, full of body. Then came his pride and joy, a 1987 Montes Alpha Cabernet Sauvignon—a truly masterly offering. I thought I spied Winnie the Pooh again, and Christopher Robin too on their way to see Owl. They were followed by Piglet carrying a picnic basket which he dropped with a puff and a grunt, before proceeding to lay out a table cloth.

There were two or three other people gathered for lunch on our side of the river. One of them I didn't get to talk to, a young wine student, but the other, a sort of Wilfred Pickles dressed in Middle East issue clothes, with a Northern English face and a studied English accent turned out to be French. He was a retired military aircraft salesman (French Mirage jets to the Middle East). So that's where they go in the winter time, these shadowy figures who feed the strife and tragedy of others. They lurk with elegant impunity at tasting lunches in dreamlike splendour.

Our hostess, Señora Grand, rings her little bell and the next course is served. The Grands have been together 35 years and they obviously run a comfortable operation. Pedro crafts woodwork of the highest quality and has knocked up all of their exquisite antiques himself. When they realise what I do for Oddbins, their sumptuous Visitors' Book was produced for me to be let loose on. I foolishly got bogged down trying to capture something of the *Wind in the Willows* magic all around us. I started with a ball point and fountain pen. So far so good, then impulsively I pour a half glass of wine over the page— the improvement didn't last long and dribbled off the page and down the book's solid wad of virgin paper. My host looks

nervous. I need colour, I explain. Don't worry— it's not finished yet. He smiles wanly, like someone who has just swallowed an oyster for the first time and is asked if he liked it.

Pedro was looking pretty sick at his posh new book. Anna produced a polythene carrier bag full of watercolours, pens and inks. I fumbled expertly and opened up a box of watercolours, called for water and pursued a line of hopeless endeavour which normally I would have abandoned long ago and started again. But this was Pedro's new book and Pedro was expecting magic. Someone brought me a cup of coffee so that went on to Pedro's book too. Who knows, this may be the stuff of magic. Mrs Grand came over and was obviously an expressionist freak. She loved the effects of moving pools of Cabernet Sauvignon and black coffee. Pedro relaxed.

26th February 1992
We met Thierry Villard, a wine maker who has spent the last 15 years making wine in Australia and is now back in Chile to make a go of it with his own wines. Thierry has thrown his energy into salvaging the best of the old and replacing the irredeemable. During 1988 to 1991, the progressive improvement in the wines, thanks to good hygiene and the use of stainless steel, is astonishing. The raw material, the grapes, are obviously superb. He considers himself one of the lucky 'starters' in Chile, in on the ground floor with the growing popularity of Chilean wines.

He had some rather odd political notions and believed the Allende government reforms of the early 1970s to have been a debacle. Maybe. When Allende expropriated land he must have incurred the wrath of the few who owned everything and won the respect of the many who had previously had nothing. Thierry Villard believes that when the farm workers were each given their small *parcellas* of land and told to get on with it, they simply adopted the attitude of their previous bosses and said, and I quote, 'I am an owner now, my boss never used to work [since the worker didn't actually see him toiling the earth] so I don't work anymore. I'll stay at home, throw a few seeds in the ground and that's it.' Within two years Chile had no food.

Thierry feels you can't just take a sub-culture of uneducated people and expect them to make things work. In that he may be right, but it appears that someone didn't want it to work, and if some of the workers had a sloppy attitude, they can only have learned by example from their previous bosses. They were meant to fail. Nobody showed them what to do and Allende would be proved wrong. Thierry feels that things were good under Pinochet. Pinochet created a free economy again, and the previous landowners bought back their lands from the workers who went bust not knowing how to become capitalists. Or those who did learn bought their neighbours' land for knockdown prices and re-employed them as workers. It had all come full circle. The elite were back in the saddle and labour was cheap again. A new entrepreneurial spirit was born and exploitation created a new wealth—for the few, the same few, and maybe a few others smart enough to climb aboard and play the game. And such 'stable economies' encourage foreign investment, bigger profits and a controlled workforce, at a price, of the same people—the eternally dispossessed, who as far as I could see never benefit from those profits. There is a dire need for schools and hospitals in Chile. That's always good for a start. Priorities are the last things on people's minds in times of growth and prosperity.

'Some people never change', says Thierry. 'You give them double pay and they still come back for a loan half-way through the month.' It seems to me that some people are not allowed to change. It's bad for business. Thierry says people just don't do what they are told. The Chileans are set in their ways, but Thierry says, they are learning.

28th February 1992
Today, we are moving north up the Pan-American Highway. The day started well. Anna had packed in the early hours for some restless reason and quite by accident committed an act of mindless terrorism. She packed my carefully blended stash of whisky with a basic Knockando foundation. Somehow, the cork was not in the bottle, even though the bottle was in its box. The whole lot glugged into our underwear, and whatever else was in what we euphemistically call our overnight

CHILEAN Wine Tasting
Vina LOS NOGALES and MONTES. (It was like a Scene f.

IN THE WILLOWS'.
Ralph STEADman

bag. In the lobby we could disguise it no longer. My breath smelt of garlic from the plate of baby eels I had consumed the night before and the lobby reeked like a wino's doorway. Now I am in a state of shock.

The journey does its best to distract me. There are mountains from one end to the other: the horizon of the whole of Chile is a mountain range. Goats are reared here among the rocky desert terrain, living off the tough scrub. Then they are slaughtered and offered for sale to passing motorists. We pass a river, and the locals offer crayfish by the side of the road. We pass a series of rubbery-looking mountains, called the Angels' Trampoline, which appear to fold in on themselves like perished sponges.

We cross a gasping desert region beyond Vallenar. (Vallenar itself is a verdant valley forming a central oasis in an otherwise arid wilderness.) As the sun dropped in the west, the red landscape burned, glowed and glowered in the diminishing light. When the sun dropped out of sight, the sky flamed like a giant oven and its light became the inner light of the endless Andes range.

Tiny shacks, the personification of frightening loneliness, stood out like protests. The shacks declared the futile defiance of man against the odds. Lights glowed from within, telling us that someone existed inside these pathetic pieces of real estate like mice in discarded packing cases. How a human being can endure such desolation and still find a reason for living is too oppressive to understand. Maybe Moses led his people to this place and not to the Holy Land. Some left, but a few stalwart believers stayed. Their scattered descendants remained in their promised land, waiting for salvation.

29th February 1992
An early morning swim set the mood for this leap year day. Today we will reach the Atacama Desert, the object of our journey. The conquistadors had travelled this whole expanse and survived to conquer.

Just between Caldera and Chañaral we came across an extraordinary shrine among gargantuan rock forms, like a giant graveyard. The shrine of Santa Gemita had steps to its top with crude radiating sticks and a flag. A cross had been fashioned out of wood and old car number plates painted silver, creating a rich patina of shapes miraculously avoiding the kitsch that religious shrines often employ to express belief or sanctity. The place emanated an aura of mystery and dark ages. The stones had many eyes and many faces. The spirits of the stones spoke sombre thoughts; walking between them animated their shapes. It was nature's own sculpture exhibition. Both God and the Devil were at the opening.

We entered the real desert in the height of the afternoon. The bleached aridity shone and glistened in the sun and smouldered in a dust-and-ochre haze. Vultures glided aimlessly along the single goods rail track, black against the light ochre. You can see them for miles—and they can see you.

The earth turns redder and scorched, rather like the inside of a furnace where the fire stones have been burned in different shades of temperature. The shapes get deeper and fold into rucks, holding their shape from the time they first cooled and lost any fluidity for eternity.

In the mid-afternoon heat, the Valley of the Moon drew us inexorably towards it, but only because we had decided to go there. The road became a sharp-edged track and a craggy, rock-formed access. In a four-wheel-drive jeep with thick tyres there was a 50/50 chance that you could make the journey back again. In a two-wheel-drive Honda with thin treads, your chances of a return journey to some form of life on earth were reduced to a 5–7 against bet, with odds in your favour. Only because the bookies would feel sure that they would never see you again. That's the trouble with bookies. They never take account of the rank outsider and throughout a good month can lose half their profits.

The only thing that made the journey seem like a reasonable risk was the confidence of our driver, Douglas Murray, who hailed from these parts, and the certain knowledge that there was actually life at the end of this stone track in a village called San Pedro de Atacama. All around us the landscape said 'No'. No, there was nothing beyond here, nothing but what you see, nothing but the brutal denial of warm existence. Not even the odd scorpion or a lean snake with an interesting bite.

The real problem, however, is the landscape. Its changing forms are so diverse that you feel sure that just round the corner there is another surprise that makes the whole tortuous experience worthwhile. There is nothing else, but there is a multitude of difference. The shapes are profuse and mind-warping. Your mind transports you to the surface of the moon and, to maintain your sanity throughout the kaleidoscopic battering, you think of Mars, too. We assume there is no life on Mars, simply because our spacecraft landed on a bit of

Mars that looked like this. It is easy to convince yourself that there is nothing else. Nothing has moved since the dawn of time. If you throw a rock, you have probably violated a piece of earth which has not moved since then. Except, perhaps, for the Indian who sits in the sun and polishes the dust off a pure chunk of crystal in the hope of a sale to someone wild enough to venture so far. The strangest thing is that you cannot even find it in you to say 'Buenos Días' and neither can he—both linger inside a natural acceptance of the other's presence. Neither of you should be there, if you had any sense.

The fact is, you are both there, a living testament to each other's existence, and while he has grown used to such weirdness you have only just begun to absorb the desolation. There is no sanctuary here, nor pity. You are alone, even with friends. You are alone with the unthinkable thoughts which you cannot shut out. This is no picnic site. This is the end. You are face to face with nature's absolute disregard for you or your well-being. You are there on account of your own impulses and you are there to test yourself against the pressure of loneliness that such a desert exerts.

Through a rock entrance you turn a corner and there before you, shimmering in the heat, are the three wise men turned to stone—a configuration of rocks so-called because of their similarity to figures about to utter words of advice like 'Go while you still can'. But the strangeness of the myriad changes and constant variety of rock forms draws you in. Sulphurous shades and an almost suffocating dryness hypnotize the brain. Breathing is short and difficult. The air is hot and thin. Odd gusts of desert wind whine mysteriously in the quietness. Some way off a whirlwind goes by, an intangible moving shape on the landscape.

Complex attempts at creative photography occupy my mind best and I fiddle with filters, smear inks on to clear plastic and complicate the vision in front of my eyes. Random experiments, impulsive and extreme, are merely a confused response to something already too weird to improve upon. But to try, just because I was there, was all that mattered. A photograph is too fundamentally literal, a matter-of-fact record of natural fiction. What I was seeing can never feel like reality, particularly afterwards. I will never believe it completely. It will always be a dream, a walk on the wildest side of nature. An idiosyncratic protest against itself inside its darkest, bleakest moments, disgorging a rare beauty from the secret, most intimate caverns of impossibility.

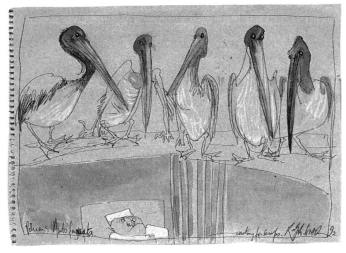